Words of Wisdom: Thirty-Six Days of Torah

Rabbi Judy Caplan Ginsburgh

Copyright © 2014 Rabbi Judy Caplan Ginsburgh

All rights reserved

ISBN: 1-885711-29-8
ISBN-13: 978-1-885711-29-8

DEDICATION

This book is dedicated to my parents, Edwin and Jacque Caplan who supported me on this journey to become a rabbi. You have always believed in me and made me feel like there was nothing I could not achieve if I tried. I also dedicate this to my family -- my husband Bob and three children, Rachel, Aaron and Jonathan who allowed me the freedom to pursue my dreams. I can only wish the same for all of you.

This book contains thirty six Divrei Torah (sermons or commentaries on the Torah and Jewish life) and my Rabbinic thesis which were written as part of the requirements to complete my program of Rabbinic studies at JSLI (Jewish Spiritual Leaders Institute). They are offered in alphabetical order. The music notes (♪ ♪) indicate brief portions of songs I shared within the sermon.

The other 16 people in my class were amazing to study with and learn from. I am grateful to each of them for their wisdom and encouragement. Thank you Art, Billy, David, Elyakim, Gabbi, Jeff, Jenn, Karen, Philip, Reuven, Rosalie, Rose, Seth, Shelly, Wolff and Zev.

I also wish to thank Rabbi Stephen Blane, Carole and Megan of the Jewish Spiritual Leaders Institute for their dedication to training and educating a new generation of rabbis.

CONTENTS

1	Balak (Ma Tovu)	8
2	Bamidbar (Everyone Counts)	9
3	B'ha-alotecha (Upside Down Nuns)	11
4	Chayei Sarah (Family is Family)	13
5	Chukkat (Mayim)	15
6	Jewish Achievement	16
7	Sukkot	19
8	Emor (The Jewish Calendar)	20
9	Jack's Bar Mitzvah	22
10	JSLI	24
11	Kedoshim (The Golden Rule)	25
12	Ki Tisa (Shavat Vayinafash)	27
13	L'chi Lach (Comfort)	29
14	Mishpatim (Acceptance)	30
15	Naso (Offerings and Blessings)	32
16	Noach (Rainbows)	24
17	Pesach (The Number Four)	36
18	Rosh Hashanah (Destroy, Define or Develop)	38
19	Shabbat	39

20	Shabbat Shira	40
21	Shelach L'cha (Tallitot)	43
22	Shemini (Faith)	45
23	Simchat Torah (To Everything There is a Season)	47
24	Spelling Bee (K-N-A-I-D-E-L)	48
25	Tazria Metzora (Balance)	49
26	Terumah (A Holy Place)	51
27	Tetzaveh (Clothes Make the Man)	53
28	Thanksgivukkah 2013	55
29	V'yak-hel Pekudey (Chazak, Chazak)	57
30	Vayeishev (Our Unique Gifts)	58
31	Vayera (There's Always Room for One More)	60
32	Vayetze (We Are All Human)	61
33	Vayigash (Seventy Ways to Look at Torah)	63
34	Vayishlach (I Have All)	64
35	Yizkor (Everyone Has A Name)	65
36	Yom Kippur D'var (Each Day is Special)	67
37	Rabbinic Thesis: Nurturing Our Souls	69

BALAK (MA TOVU)

♪♪ *Ma tovu ohalecha Ya'akov, mishk'notecha Yisra'el*

The musical setting of *Ma Tovu* by Danny Maseng is perhaps one of my favorites. Not only is it a beautiful and lush melody to sing, but it also captures the feeling expressed in the words "How good are your tents, O Jacob, your dwelling places O Israel!" These words were first uttered by Balaam, a non-Jew who is often compared to Haman and Hitler. In this week's Torah portion, Balaam is hired by King Balak to curse the Israelites. He attempts to curse them three different times, but when he speaks, blessings pour from his mouth instead of curses. In Numbers chapter 24, verse 5, Balaam is set to utter the third curse. But, he is so overcome with awe at God and the site of the Tabernacle and tents of the Israelites that the words *"Ma tovu ohalecha Ya'akov, mishk'notecha Yisra'el"* come out instead. *Ma Tovu* is a prayer that we recite each day at the beginning of the morning liturgy upon entering the synagogue. How could a blessing written by a non-Jew who wanted to curse the Jewish people become so basic to each Jewish day?

There have been many commentaries written speculating about what Balaam saw as he gazed out over the tents of the Israelites. According to Rashi, Balaam observed that the tents of the Israelites were not directly facing each other, indicating a degree of privacy for each home. So, no one was minding the business of or gossiping about their neighbor. It could be said that we say *Ma Tovu* at the beginning of daily prayer to remind us that we are in the synagogue for prayer and not to worry about what our neighbor is wearing or doing.

According to another commentary, Balaam saw tents that not only provided shelter, comfort and protection, but they were also places to gather, pray, study and connect with others and with God. Ron Wolfson writes that when we compare a good synagogue with a good tent, "The spirituality of welcoming begins with hospitality that brings people closer to each other, to community, to Judaism, and to God." Perhaps Balaam's blessing signified a hope for what our modern day Jewish tents should be. Our sanctuaries should be open and inviting to all and should connect us more deeply with Adonai. Each morning when we say *Ma Tovu* we are stating how glad we are to be members of this tribe as we express a sense of belonging to a community.

Karen Kushner makes a beautiful metaphor about *Mah Tovu*. She asks us to visualize everyone getting ready for prayer in the morning before reciting *Mah Tovu*. We see everyone putting on their *tallit*. They are putting the prayer shawls over their heads immersed in their own private ritual making their own personal tents. Perhaps this is what Balaam saw as an outsider as he looked out over the Israelite encampment. He saw individual tents which together made a whole community. How good are our tents and our dwelling places that our traditions continue to live on in Jewish communities throughout the world. Amen.

BAMIDBAR (EVERYONE COUNTS)

This week's Torah portion is the first portion of the book of Numbers and is called *Bamidbar*, which means "desert". *Bamidbar* is always read on the Shabbat before Shavuot, which celebrates the giving of the Torah. In this portion, we read of the census taken of the Jewish people by Moses.

A census conveys two paradoxical truths. On one hand, it implies that each individual person is significant. On the other hand, a census or head-count is the ultimate equalizer showing that each member of the community, from the greatest to the meekest, counts for no less and no more than "one."

Once there was a small town which consisted of only a few Jewish families. Between all the families, they had exactly ten men over the age of bar mitzvah. They were all dedicated people and they made sure that they never missed a *minyan*. One day, a new Jewish family moved in to town. There was great joy and excitement because now they would have eleven men. But a strange thing happened. As soon as they had eleven, they could never manage to have a *minyan*!

The moral of the story is: When we know we are indispensable, we make a point of being there.

In a *minyan*...everyone counts. It does not matter how learned you are, how much money you give to the synagogue, or - in our Reform tradition - whether you are male or female. We all count equally. If we count Jews because every Jew counts, then this implies a responsibility on Jewish communal leaders to ensure that no Jew is missing from the greater community. It implies a responsibility to make sure everyone feels that they belong and are welcome -- even if they haven't paid their dues, even if they did not attend a special event, even if they are searching for more Jewish knowledge.

Congregations need to embrace the individual qualities of their members. In God's eyes, we are all equal, but we all possess special gifts that are unique to us. Jewish communities should take the time to find out what special talents and gifts their members have to offer. Communities should create opportunities for and encourage members to share, teach and be appreciated for what they uniquely bring to the community. The statement, "you are never a prophet in your own land" does not have to be true. Instead of always looking for better things outside of our community, maybe we should look harder right here at home. Just like the Jews who wandered for 40 years in the desert....they were stuck with each other. There was nowhere else to go. They, like small Jewish communities of today, were isolated and insulated. They had to learn to make the most with what they had. They had to learn to appreciate what they had. They had to learn to accept their fellow Jews as partners in community.

Not only do the leaders of our Jewish community have a responsibility to make our community welcoming and nurturing, but each individual Jew has certain commitments and obligations as well. Each one of us is an important part of this community. Each one of us has wisdom, talents, experience and gifts to share.

So don't get lost wandering in your own desert. Your Jewish community needs you.

Next week, we celebrate the giving of the Torah to the Jewish people on Mount Sinai. In the Torah, every letter counts. One missing letter invalidates the entire scroll. Likewise, one missing Jew leaves a Jewish community lacking and incomplete. May we follow the example of our ancestors who wandered in the desert and learn to appreciate what we have right here at home while always striving for a land (or community) of promise. Amen.

B'HA-ALOTECHA (UPSIDE DOWN NUNS)

This week's Torah portion is from the 3rd book of Numbers (Bamidbar) and is called *B'ha-alotecha* which means "when you step up" or in this case "when you mount" referring to God's instructions to Aaron about "mounting" the lamps of the *menorah* in the Tabernacle. This Torah portion begins with these instructions on lighting the *menorah* and continues with instructions for purifying the Levite workers, preparations for the departure from Sinai and then lots of complaining and whining from the Jewish people while they are journeying in the desert.

But, there is something very curious and unique in this Torah portion that you would never know unless you looked at the Hebrew. In this Torah portion, two verses of Chapter 10 (verses 35 and 36) are somewhat set apart from the rest of the text. Similar to the beginning of a new book of Torah, there is lots of space surrounding these two verses. And even more interesting is the appearance of two upside down Hebrew letter *"nuns"* – one appears prior to verse 35 and one appears at the end of verse 36. This is only place in the entire Torah where these upside down *"nuns"* appear. The question is, why are they there and what do they mean?

The simple answer is, we really don't know. However, there has been lots of speculation which is very fascinating. The two verses that are set apart by the upside down "*nuns*" translate as, "When the ark was to set out, Moses would say: Advance, O Lord! May Your enemies be scattered, and may Your foes flee before You! And when it halted, he would say: Return, O Lord, You who are Israel's myriads of thousands!"

According to the Talmud, these upside down "*nuns*" indicate that these two verses of the Torah are out of place. Some say the upside down "*nuns*" were the precursors of our modern parentheses. It has been suggested that the two verses in question should follow Numbers, Chapter 2, verse 17 which talks about the Tabernacle being moved and how the various tribes are to march in position.

Rabbi Yehudah ha-Nasi says that the upside down "*nuns*" are not error marks, but instead indicate that these two verses are actually a separate book of Torah all on their own. If this is true, it would mean that there are really three Books of Numbers – the book of Numbers before chapter 10 verses 35-36; the short 85 letter book contained in verses 35-36; and the rest of the book of Numbers. (It is interesting to note that the minimum number of letters a text has to have in order to be saved from fire because of its holiness or to be considered a complete book, is 85.) If this speculation is true, then our Torah would have seven books and not five.

A third scenario suggests that the upside down "*nuns*" represent the two Hebrew words beginning with the letter "*nun*" that were proclaimed by the Israelites when they stood at the foot of Sinai before receiving the Torah: "*Na-a-she v'Nishma*" - "we will do and we will listen". These words declared the Jewish people's spiritual connection to God. However, just one year later their desire for a quick departure from Sinai and their complaining to God, were a rejection of that declaration of words beginning with the letter "*nun*". These two negative reactions by the Israelites proceed and follow the two verses surrounded by the upside down "*nuns*". Thus, the upside down "*nuns*" could signify that this initial proclamation to God had been flipped upside down.

A fourth explanation offered by a Chabad Rabbi suggests that the upside down *"nuns"* stand for the words *"niglah"* (the revealed Torah) and *"nistor"* (the concealed Torah). The Five Books of Moses, or Torah as we know it, is known as the Written Law. But, Moses was given both the Written Law and the Oral Law on Mt. Sinai. The revealed and concealed Torah are both part of this Oral Law. The *"niglah"* or revealed Torah is what we call the Talmud. The *"nistor"* or concealed Torah is what we call Kabbalah. These two upside down *"nuns"* could have been placed here to make sure we do not forget that there is more to Torah and our study than just the Five Books of Moses that were given to us on Mount Sinai. As Jews, it is our responsibility to constantly study and analyze the meanings of the Torah in all its forms.

And a final explanation for these two upside down *"nuns"* is that they represent the word *"ner"* which means light in Hebrew. This Torah portion begins with instructions to Aaron on how to light the menorah in the Tabernacle. The concept of lighting a candle fulfills a mitzvah. The flame of the candle represents knowledge. Aaron was commanded to ignite this spark so that we could fulfill the mitzvah of studying Torah.

So, why are these upside down *"nuns"* placed here? We will never truly know, but some of the theories offered attempt to shed light on this puzzle and certainly provide us with interesting material for further study and conversation.

CHAYEI SARAH (FAMILY IS FAMILY)

This week's Torah portion, *Chayei Sarah*, begins with the death of our first Matriarch, Sarah and ends with the death of our first, Patriarch, Abraham.

As I read the portion, something really stuck out to me…something I wanted to find out more about. In Chapter 25, verse 9, it reads, "His sons Isaac and Ishmael buried him in the cave of Machpelah…" Whoa, wait a minute, since when did Isaac and Ishmael get together? Earlier in Genesis, Abraham banishes Hagar and Ishmael into the wilderness and we do not hear about them again. And there is no mention of Isaac being at Sarah's burial. So, where was he? It is often out of a sense of family or religious obligation that people are brought together to bury their dead. Is this what happened in the case of Isaac and Ishmael? Or had the two brothers made up and come to terms with how their father, Abraham had treated them? So many questions, so few answers.

If we look closely at Genesis, we realize that Isaac does not return with Abraham after the *Akedah*. In fact, the next time we hear about Isaac is in Genesis chapter 24, verse 62, when he sees his future wife, Rebecca. In this chapter, we are told that, "Isaac had just come back from the vicinity of *B'eir lachai roi*." This place is mentioned earlier in Genesis (chapter 16, verse 13) after Hagar runs away because she has been treated so poorly by Sarah. When God speaks to Hagar, she calls God "*El –roi.*" The well where she speaks to God becomes known as *B'eir lachai roi* meaning "the well of the living One who sees me." This place is mentioned one other time in this portion (chapter 25, verse 11). "After the death of Abraham, God blessed his son Isaac and Isaac settled near *B'eir lachai roi.*"

The *midrash* offers some very interesting explanations. Some feel that when Hagar and Ishmael were banished by Abraham, they went back to the well where God had spoken to Hagar at *B'eir lachai roi*. And, later we read that Isaac returned from *B'eir lachai roi* when he meets Rebecca. Perhaps, Isaac goes to be with his brother after almost being killed by his father. Part of the *midrash* even goes so far as to say that one of the two servants who accompanied Abraham and Isaac when they went up to Mt. Moriah was Ishmael. It seems to make sense that Isaac and Ishmael were possibly living together when their father died.

At the end of the portion, we also learn that Abraham remarries a woman named Keturah. According to a *midrash*, this woman was Hagar. Perhaps they were all together when Abraham died….Hagar, Ishmael and Isaac. We will never really know, but what fascinating information to ponder.

Putting all of this speculation aside, it was nice to see that two brothers came together once again to bury their father and to end the rivalry that existed between them. My hope is that Isaac and Ishmael and even Abraham all did reconcile before Abraham's death. This is how it should be in families. We should be willing to forgive and make the most of each day we have in this life with those who are the most precious to us. Amen.

CHUKKAT (MAYIM)

♪♪ *Spring up, O well!*

Oh, the water in the well and the healing in the well
The women and the water and the hope that's in the well.

This Shabbat, we read from *Parsha Chukkat* and within this portion, we learn of the death of Miriam. Throughout her life of over 100 years, Miriam is associated over and over again with water. And curiously, Miriam's name is closely related to the Hebrew word for water – *Mayim*. We first hear of Miriam (without knowing her name) as a woman who pulled her baby brother from the River Nile and brought him to safety in the palace of the Pharoah. Another significant time we read about Miriam in the Torah is when she led the women in song and rejoicing after the Jews escaped slavery by triumphantly crossing the Red Sea. And, when we read of Miriam for the final time, (in this Torah portion) it is about her death. We learn that after Miriam dies, the rock which provided water for the Israelites as they journeyed through the desert has dried up and disappeared among the other rocks of the desert. It is at this point that the Israelites realize that Miriam is the source of the water. It is not until Miriam is gone, that the people realize how truly vital she was.

Rashi tells us that, because of Miriam's integrity and caring for the Jewish people, the Israelites and their animals were provided with water to nourish their bodies in the desert. To not have had water would have proved fatal. If it had not been for Miriam's "well" no one would have heard the words of Moses or made it to the Promised Land.

Miriam is one of the few women mentioned in the Torah on her own merit. Yes, she is the older sister of both Moses and Aaron, but she is also respected as a leader and a prophet among the Jewish people. Miriam was a woman of deeds, not words. She is known more for what she did, rather than what she said. Miriam practiced and shared the words of the Torah with her people. Through Torah, she provided them with spiritual sustenance for their minds and their souls. And it is exceedingly appropriate that the water which provided sustenance for the Israelites in the desert is associated with Miriam as well. Miriam was a source through which our ancestors were provided with sustenance for mind, body and spirit. She sets a wonderful example for all women to follow – mothers, daughters and sisters; teachers, caregivers and healers; and all women who make our families, our communities and our world a better place. May their wells of support, compassion and sustenance continue to flow as Miriam's legacy to us all. Amen.

JEWISH ACHIEVEMENT

In 2009, a Presbyterian man named Steven Pease, published a book titled, "The Golden Age of Jewish Achievement." Steven Pease was born in 1943 in Spokane, Washington. As he says, he grew up "sympathetic to Jews" through reading books like "The Diary of Anne Frank", hearing of the atrocities of the Holocaust, and watching the hit movie, "Exodus" starring Paul Newman. To young Steven Pease, Jews were the underdogs, the victims who responded to their oppression by creating their own country. There were not many Jews where he grew up in Spokane, but at University of Washington and Harvard Business School, where he received his education, he met and admired many Jewish students and mentors. As he made his way in the business world, negotiating deals and serving on many boards of directors, he met and gained a healthy respect for Jews. These encounters and partnerships led him to ask the question: It seemed that Jews were disproportionately high achievers and contributors. Is this really true?

So, as Steven Pease puts it, he became "a Gentile working on a PhD in Jewish Studies." His book, "The Golden Age of Jewish Achievement" documents his findings and attempts to answer this question.

Statistics tell us that there are approximately fifteen million Jews in a world of six billion people. To put this in perspective, Jews are so few in number that in a room of 1,000 people representing the world's total population, only 2 would be Jewish. The facts show that 23% of all the Nobel Peace Prizes ever awarded have gone to Jews. Of the 521 Nobel Prizes awarded for sciences, Jews have won 137. Thirty seven percent of movie directors who have won Oscars are Jews. Twenty six percent of those receiving Kennedy Center Honors and fourteen percent of the Grammy Lifetime Achievement Award recipients are Jews. Fifty one percent of the Pulitzer Prizes for nonfiction writing have gone to Jews. Jews account for roughly thirty percent of the faculty of Harvard, Stanford and Yale law schools. Jews pioneered the ready to wear garment business, and as early as 1885, owned all but seven of New York's 241 garment factories. Levi Strauss, Ralph Lauren, Calvin Klein, Estee Lauder, Macy's, Neiman-Marcus, Bloomingdale's, Sears, Gap, Home Depot, QVC, Starbucks, Ben & Jerry's, Weight Watchers, Jenny Craig, Hyatt, Royal Caribbean…like the Adam Sandler song – All Jews! And let us not forget sports – Jews own twenty nine percent of the NFL football teams and forty percent of the NBA basketball teams. Even on Broadway, Jews excel. Thirty eight of the fifty longest running Broadway shows are musicals and of those thirty eight, twenty four (63%) were written by Jews.

So what is behind the talent and drive that leads to this disproportionate achievement? Steve Pease offers some points to consider:

Jews are the chosen people. Being "God's chosen people" might explain these amazing achievements had it not been for the unbelievable hardships Jews have endured for centuries. Another way of looking at the word "chosen" is that Jews were chosen by God for the special responsibility of *tikkun olam* or repairing the world for the benefit of all humankind. And Pease points to the **culture** of Judaism as being the most important factor in our remarkable achievements. The Random House Dictionary defines culture as, "the behaviors and beliefs characteristic of a particular social, ethnic or age group." According to Pease, Jewish culture and tradition teaches us:

1) That actions have consequences
2) That we must take responsibility for ourselves
3) That we are allowed to question and have opposing views, thus we are often more tolerant of others
4) That we are encouraged to speak out and speak well (as evidenced by our Bar/Bat Mitzvah right of passage)
5) That a good education with advanced degrees is important (ask any Jewish mother)
6) That we have an obligation to pass on our beliefs and traditions to our children
7) That in order to earn a living, Jews had to be creative, even entrepreneurial and autonomous because we came up against so many barriers
8) That high achievement and excellence were a ticket to respect
9) That Jews, from the time of Abraham, have been different, and in being different, we have learned tenacity and have overcome negative stereotypes through superior performance
10) That money is a tool for providing charity

In short, our culture, our traditions, the way we have been raised and the values that we, as Jews, hold high are what contribute the most to our outstanding achievements through the ages. As Mark Twain is quoted as saying, "Properly, the Jew ought hardly to be heard of, but he is heard of, has always been heard of. He is as prominent on the planet as any other people, and his ... contributions are [way] out of proportion to the weakness of his numbers." Amen.

SUKKOT

♪♪ *Lulav Shake (by Steve Dropkin)*

Sukkot is a harvest holiday
The celebration lasts for seven days
We build our sukkah, then we decorate
A special booth in which we congregate. Do the lulav shake...

The symbols of sukkot are quite unique
They show God's presence the entire week
The etrog's smell it gets into the air
We wave the lulav everywhere. Do the lulav shake.....

Hadas and aravah on either side
Surround the lulav that we shake with pride
To north, the south, the west and to the east
We celebrate and then we feast. Do the lulav shake...

As the song says, "the symbols of sukkot are quite unique." Sukkot is a holiday which celebrates the harvest, but as many Midrashim suggest, the symbols of Sukkot - known as the *Arba Minim* or the four species - can teach us much about sharing, community and unity. In these symbols, we see diversity and differences coming together to form a whole unit.

First, we have the *etrog*, a citron which takes almost an entire year to ripen on the tree. The *etrog* grows primarily in the plains of Israel. The Midrash tells us that the *etrog* represents our human heart and has both a good taste and a good smell, symbolizing Jews who study Torah and do *mitzvot*.

The next symbol, the *lulav* is the branch of a date palm which grows in the deserts of Israel. The lulav represents our spine. It has taste but no smell, symbolizing Jews who study Torah but do not do *mitzvot*.

The *hadas* or myrtle grows in the mountains of Israel. It represents our eyes and has a good smell, but no taste, symbolizing Jews who do *mitzvot*, but do not study Torah.

And the fourth symbol, the *aravah* or willow branch grows in the river valleys of Israel. It represents our mouths. The willow possesses neither a good smell nor a good taste and symbolizes Jews who neither study Torah nor do *mitzvot*.

On Sukkot, when we bring these four species together, we are literally bringing together items from four diverse ecological habitats Israel. Symbolically, we are bringing together various parts of our bodies and various types of Jews. In doing so, according to the Midrash, we are creating a whole person and a whole community. It takes all kinds of people to form a community. A healthy community is one that is willing to learn, share, respect and support one another. May our community be like the symbols of Sukkot unifying itself with inclusion, sharing, respect and support. Amen.

EMOR (THE JEWISH CALENDAR)

This week's Torah portion is called *Emor*, which in Hebrew means "speak." This portion contains 63 of the 613 commandments God gave the Jewish people. In Chapter 23 of *Emor*, Adonai tells Moses to tell the Israelites about the "fixed times" which are to be observed as sacred occasions. Adonai instructs Moses on how we should celebrate special holy days and festivals throughout the Jewish calendar. Adonai begins by saying that for six days of each week, we may work, but on the seventh day, there will be a Sabbath of complete rest. We next discover that the first month of the Jewish calendar is actually *Nisan* and not *Tishrei* when *Rosh Hashanah* falls. Adonai outlines the major festivals beginning with the one falling on "the fifteenth day of the first month" which is Passover. Adonai commands that we are to eat "unleavened cakes" for a 7 day period and that the 1st and 7th days are to be holy with no work of labor on them. This holiday period symbolizes our freedom from bondage. On the second evening of this festival, we are to bring an *omer* – a measure of barley – to the high priest to signify the beginning of the reaping or harvest period. And we are to count this *omer* for the next seven weeks culminating on the 50th day with the holy day of *Shavuot* celebrating the giving of the Torah. The portion goes on to mention other holy days in our calendar – *Rosh Hashanah* where the shofar shall be sounded, *Yom Kippur* where you shall atone and practice self-denial, and *Sukkot* where you shall live in booths. Several times throughout this listing of festivals and holy occasions, Adonai mentions that "this is an eternal statute throughout your generations in all your dwelling places."

There is a Chassidic story about a king and his son. They were traveling in the desert with the royal entourage and the young prince became very thirsty. He asked his father, the king, for water. The king immediately ordered his servants to dig a well. By the end of the day, they had found water which seeped up through the well. The son's thirst was quenched. Later, the son asked his father why he had made his servants work so hard to dig a well when they could have just sent someone to the nearest town to bring back some water. The king replied, "My son, right now we have the resources to dig a well. But one day, you may not have as much and this well will be here for that time when you or your children may need water." "But father," said the prince, "in many years, the sands of time will refill the well, stopping its water and erasing its memory!"

"My son," said the king, "you are right, so this is what we will do. We will mark the site of this well on our maps. If you know the exact spot at which this well has been sunk, you will be able to reopen it with little effort and toil." Then the king resolved, "We will dig wells all along our travel route and mark their places on our map. We will record the particular characteristics of each well and the method by which it can be reopened. So whenever you or your children will travel this route, you will be able to obtain the water that will sustain you on your journey."

Just as the king dug wells of water all along his journey, the Jewish calendar is our map and guide through God's festivals and holy days. The calendar provides us with "wells" or traditions to nurture our spiritual journeys. As we travel through each year with every new generation, we celebrate these special holy days which become spiritual wells to nurture our souls. Each of these festivals has its own characteristics and observances. We must celebrate and share the customs and traditions of these festivals each year with our families. For, in doing so, we ensure the continuation of Judaism for future generations and we keep our eternal statute with our God. Amen.

JACK'S BAR MITZVAH

In May, 2013, I had the pleasure of officiating at the Bar Mitzvah of Jack Noles. Jack is an exceptional young man who studied hard for his Bar Mitzvah and was very conscious of wanting to make a difference in the world with the planting of a garden at our Temple. This is the *D'var* that I gave on the Friday night prior to his Bar Mitzvah.

It is always so interesting to me how Torah portions really fit the person they are assigned to. Your Torah portion, *B'har*, could not have been more appropriate for you. Many of you know that Jack has planted a beautiful garden of vegetables and trees outside our Temple. And, he will continue to tend that garden and harvest its fruits. Tomorrow, when you finish the reading of your Torah portion, you will say the words, "*Chazak, chazak, v'nithazeik*" – be strong, be strong and we will strengthen one another. This phrase is said every time we complete a book of the Torah. Tomorrow, you will complete the book of Leviticus and next week we will begin the book of Numbers.

Again, it is no mistake that we say these words on the occasion of your Bar Mitzvah. The word *chazak*, which we translate here to mean "be strong" is actually an acronym for three different Hebrew words:

Harisha which means plowing

Z'reah which means planting

K'tzirah which means harvesting

Before planting a garden, you must first **plow** (*harisha*) the ground to prepare the earth. Then you are ready to **plant** (*z'reah*) seeds and nurture them until they grow. Unless you take good care of the garden and tend to it almost daily, it will not yield the quality or quantity of produce you may have wished for. Ultimately, if you have done your job well, you will **harvest** (*k'tzirah*) a good crop. Plowing, planting and harvesting – *chazak*!!

Just like this example of the garden, Jack, you have studied Torah to reach this special time of becoming a Bar Mitzvah. Before you could study Torah, the foundation or groundwork for your Jewish studies had to be established. You had to learn basic Hebrew and prepare yourself for more advanced study. Your religious school teachers, your family and the rabbis you worked with planted the seeds that helped you begin your journey as a Jew. And those who studied with you had to reinforce what you were learning and you had to practice and review it time and time again. Only after this, could you harvest the fruits of your labor – what we are all witnessing this weekend.

You have been planted in your own garden of knowledge. We hope you will continue to grow and learn and gather strength from it which you will use throughout your life. In this way, you will solidify your own knowledge, you will add to the knowledge of your community and we will all become stronger from it.

We look forward to your becoming a Bar Mitzvah – a son of the commandment – tomorrow. And we look forward to celebrating this *simcha* – special occasion – with you and your family. *Chazak, chazak, v'nithazeik.* May you, Jack, continue to go from strength to strength and by continuing to grow in your Jewish knowledge and by sharing it with others, especially the next generation, may <u>you</u> be strengthened. Amen.

JSLI

Since this is our last class until after the High Holy Days, I dedicate this D'var to Rabbi Blane. Like most of us in Class #6, I thought about becoming an ordained cantor or rabbi for many years. However, it was just not possible to do in the conventional way in this lifetime. I found out about the Jewish Spiritual Leaders Institute (JSLI) from a friend – Barry Altmark -who went through the program about a year ago and is now known as the Deep South Rabbi. Barry encouraged me to look at JSLI and after a few conversations with Rabbi Blane, I decided to give it a try. I was skeptical about this online learning, about what and how I would learn. Will I really learn enough to be ordained in just a year? Will I be accepted by others in the rabbinate? Will I be considered "official" enough to serve a congregation?

I can honestly say that I have learned so much in this first six months of study. I look forward to every single assignment and every class. The world of the virtual classroom is amazing. I have met people in this class whom I know will be friends for life – and we haven't even really met. Will I learn enough in just a year? One cannot possibly know everything there is to know in order to be a rabbi in one year, in five years, or even in a lifetime. But I will learn enough to know where to go to learn more for the rest of my life.

Will I be accepted by others in the rabbinate? I have found that most of my rabbinic friends who really know and care about me, are happy for me. Most have been very encouraging about this choice. A few have had issues and feel that what we are doing at JSLI somehow "cheapens the rabbinate." I can only feel sadness for them at being so insecure with their place in Jewish life that they feel compelled to say things like this. There are good rabbis and there are those that are not as good. Just like in any profession….some are better than others. And as most of us know, it often has very little to do with how well or where you were taught. It is a calling for those who do it well and for all the right reasons. I would like to count myself in this group.

And, will I be considered "official" enough to serve a congregation? The answer is yes. I know this is something that I have worked toward my entire life. From being one of the few students who actually loved Sunday School, winning the "Best Student" award at confirmation, tutoring Hebrew and teaching in Jewish schools from the time I was 15, becoming active in Jewish educational organizations, teaching myself liturgy and a vast repertoire of melodies to become a cantorial soloist to taking the leap of enrolling at JSLI – this is all a culmination of a lifetime of Jewish learning and sharing. Yes, I <u>will</u> be official. And some congregation out there <u>will</u> value my services as their Rabbi.

Thank you, Rabbi Blane for having the foresight and courage to begin JSLI. May you continue to inspire and train rabbis for the future for many years to come.

KEDOSHIM (THE GOLDEN RULE)

This Shabbat we read one of my personal favorite Torah portions – *Kedoshim*, sometimes referred to as "the holiness code." The Hebrew word *kadosh* from which *kedoshim* is derived means "holy". This Torah portion from Leviticus chapters 19 & 20 contains some of the most quoted lines in Torah and some of our ancient teachers have taught that everything we need to know about Judaism is contained in this particular Torah portion. In our Reform tradition, this portion, *Kedoshim*, is read again during the *Yom Kippur* afternoon service. I personally feel that the essence of who we are as Jews, and human beings in general, is contained in this Torah portion. Tonight I will speak about two major quotes from the portion that sum up how we, as Jews, should strive to live our lives.

The portion begins with the first major quote. Adonai addresses Moses and tells Moses to speak to the <u>entire</u> Jewish community saying to them, *Kedoshim t'hiyu kee kadosh ani Adonai elohechem* - "You shall be holy, for I, the Lord your God, am holy." This summons by God is given in the plural and spoken to the entire community. This indicates that each and every one of us has the capacity to be holy, but we cannot be holy only on our own. The portion goes on to list various commandments – commandments we must keep with God and commandments we must keep with our fellow man. So, our holiness is dependent upon what we do and how we act when interacting with both God and with our fellow man.

We are all made *B'tzelem Elohim* – in the image of God. Jewish mysticism or *Kabbalah* teaches that we all share a common soul – *Adam ha rishon*. When man was created, all souls were contained within him. And as each individual is born, he or she is given a soul. We are all on this earth in separate, unique shells or physical bodies, but we are all connected spiritually having been made in the image of God and sharing a common soul.

The second major quote in this portion is found in Leviticus chapter 19, verse 18 and is perhaps one of the most quoted lines of Torah -- *V'ahavta l'ray-echa kamocha* which literally translates as "love your fellow as yourself." Rabbi Akiva called this the cardinal principle of the Torah. And we are all taught the story of Hillel who, when approached by a man who was not Jewish and asked to tell him everything there was to know about Judaism while he stood on one foot, Hillel replied, "What is distasteful to you, do not do to another person. This is the entire Torah, all the rest is commentary…now go and study it." This statement by Hillel has also been called, "the golden rule" and is the standard by which we should behave as moral human beings.

In order to live by this "golden rule", we must not only love ourselves, but also love our fellowman. And, we must not love someone else more or less than we love ourselves. If we are all connected to God through our souls, then we all have the capacity to love, to be loved and to be good. We can visualize this as spokes in a wheel. We all live our own individual lives in our individual bodies – these are the spokes of the wheel. At the rim or the outer part of the wheel, each spoke is disconnected and separate. But at the hub, the center, the core, all of the spokes connect. This core is our spiritual hub and spiritually, we <u>are</u> all connected. We are truly all one people – one humanity. We can selfishly begin with ourselves at the center, but we must branch out within our broader world and interact with our family, then with our Jewish community, then with our community at large, and eventually with all of humanity. One step at a time, we learn to love, accept, pardon and forgive. We learn to love our fellow -- our fellow Jews and our fellow human beings as we love ourselves and as <u>God</u> loves all of us. Amen.

KI TISA (SHAVAT VAYINAFASH)

Our Torah portion this evening is *Ki Tisa* which literally translates as "when you raise up." According to Chabad.org, the idiomatic meaning of these words is "when you take the census of the Israelites," but, the literal meaning implies that the entire contents of this Torah portion is a process through which the Jewish people become elevated to heights they would not have achieved otherwise. Yes, this portion talks about the census or counting of the Israelites, the continuing building of the sanctuary or *mishkan* and the ultimate sin of the golden calf. But what spoke to me most about this portion were the references to Shabbat as a day of rest and the obligation of Jews to observe it just as God did when the world was created.

In the book of Genesis, after the first week of creation, we read, "*uvayom hashvi'i shavat vayinafash*" — on the seventh day God ceased working and was refreshed. These words are recited or sung each Shabbat in the familiar V'shamru prayer. The word *shavat* means to cease and from this root, we get the word *Shabbat* meaning rest. The final word of the V'shamru prayer is *va-yinafash* which translates to mean "and was refreshed." It is derived from the noun – *nefesh* meaning soul, life energy or our essential character. According to the Etz Chayim Torah Commentary, the use of the verb form *va-yinafash* infers the notion of a "fresh infusion of spiritual and physical vigor and the revival of one's total being."

Scholar and author, Everett Fox takes it a step further and translates the word *va-yinafash* as "paused for breath," suggesting that God actively stopped working and actively paused to take in a much-needed breath. God did two things – stopped working and paused to take a breath. There is a mystical tradition that states that, on Shabbat, a Jew gains a *neshamah y'teyrah,* an extra soul. During Shabbat, we have the potential to be doubly, spiritually charged.

We are commanded by God to stop our work on Shabbat. Shabbat, the day of rest, is a covenant between God and the Jewish people. Shabbat allows us to recharge our physical, mental and spiritual batteries if we will only make ourselves stop. We need to find ways to make Shabbat special in our lives. And, we need to "work" in order to earn our pause from work. Only by actively stepping away from those things that define our non-Shabbat world, will our souls become refreshed. But, as Everett Fox states, it is not enough to just stop working. We must also take a breath. We can gain an extra soul. We can be doubly, spiritually charged.

Yes, we must stop working and we must rest. But, Shabbat also provides a space for us to recharge by doing things we do not do during our work week. For Reform Jews, Shabbat does not have to be a time when we stop our lives completely. But Shabbat could be a time we set aside for reflection, learning something new, visiting a new place, doing something fun with our families and yes, even praying. I urge you to try to carve out some time each Shabbat to stop working, and to take a much needed breath to discover how you and your family can make Shabbat special. Each of us has been given a weekly opportunity to energize and renew our soul, body and mind in preparation to engage in another hectic 6 days of work. If we truly think about the meaning of Shabbat in our lives, we can allow ourselves to become elevated to heights we may not have achieved otherwise. Amen.

L'CHI LACH (COMFORT)

In this Torah portion, Adonai asks Abraham to leave his home and go "to a land that I will show you." Abraham is asked to leave everything he knows, everything that makes him feel safe and secure and venture out into unknown territory. He is allowed to take his wife, Sarah, and his nephew, Lot.

This Torah portion always makes me think of the assignment we would get in school when talking about people who had to make quick evacuations from their homes because of hurricanes, tornados or fires. "If you had to leave your home in a big hurry, what (three things) would you take with you?" When I was younger and this question was posed to me, it was difficult to decide what to take and I am sure my mind changed often. We all have so much stuff. But as I get older, it is easier to know what I would take. And, having counseled people who have lost everything due to natural disasters, I have given more thought to this question in recent years. I think what I would take falls into three categories: comfort, memories and reality.

For comfort, I would take my teddy bear who has been with me my entire life. For memories, I would grab a large basket I prepared after Hurricane Katrina that contains family photo albums, baby albums and DVDs of life cycle events within our family. These would help with memories. And, my reality would be to take as many members of my family as I could. They are my reality and without them, I would not be complete.

There is a *midrash* (story) that says that God made Abraham leave because he knew he would never reach his potential if he stayed where he was. Sometimes, we are asked to take a leap of faith similar to Abraham. We must make changes in order to reach new heights. Each of us in this Rabbinic Class at JSLI has stepped out of our comfort zones to experience something new, something potentially exciting that can help us reach our true selves and our goal of being Jewish leaders. We all have faith that one day we will become Rabbis and serve our Jewish people. And that goal is looming ever closer. What have we each taken with us? And, what potential do we have the ability to reach? Change is never easy. Venturing into unknown territory can be scary. But we have all taken, not only the first step, but we are almost at the end of our journey. May we all discover new things about ourselves along this journey and may we be changed in order that we may reach our best selves. Amen.

MISHPATIM (ACCEPTANCE)

There is a *midrash* that tells that the Torah was offered by God to all the nations of the world and none accepted without first asking what the laws were about. Then once they found out, they came up with all sorts of reasons why they could not abide by them. The Israelites were the only ones who accepted the laws BEFORE knowing what they were about. And, even after Moses shared them and explained them, the Jewish people replied: "*Kol asher diber Adonai na'aseh v'nishma*" – all that Adonai says, we will do and we will obey."

The *Zohar* (a literary work of Jewish mystical thought known as *Kabbalah*) offers an interpretation of this. When we say, "we will do", we are committing ourselves to observe these laws and when we say, "we will obey", we are committing ourselves to understand and continuously study the laws. According to the teachings in the *Zohar*, these laws should be internalized and should become a part of our very essence. We, the collective Jewish people who stood at Mt. Sinai, agreed to accept and fulfill God's commandments even before we knew what they were or the impact they would have on our lives. Not only did we make a commitment to live by these laws, but we also vowed to study these laws and understand them. Through living a righteous life by following God's *mitzvot* (or commandments), we can find true spirituality. But, we cannot live a righteous life alone. Spirituality is not achieved solely through meditation or being alone. We must live our lives within a larger society. We must interpret these laws within the context of our modern world and our individual communities.

Many of the laws listed in this longer than usual *parsha* concern rules for living within a community of others. Some of these laws have been replaced by more modern secular laws and some of these laws, at face value, may no longer make sense in our modern society. So, how do we as Reform Jews interpret and live by these ancient laws given to us so many thousands of years ago. Rabbi Solomon Freehof offers a solution by stating that in our modern society, these laws "provide guidance, not governance." Dan Bridge, the Director of Hillel at University of Washington offers that, "[Judaism] encourages informed individuals to make decisions within the context of an educated community."

Being a part of this Rabbinic class gives us the opportunity to do just that. We are able to share our differing views and look at each portion of our Torah with a variety of eyes and insights. We are able to glean from the Torah the energy and the essence needed in order to live righteous lives. We have to be able to take these ancient laws and use them to help us make everyday situations holy. For example – take a glass of wine. Some may immediately think about drinking it to escape from the pressures of everyday life and some may even drink to excess. Others will look at this same glass of wine and use it to sanctify the holy day of Shabbat. It is the same sort of metaphor as – "is the glass half empty or half full?" It is all in the way we look at things, how we interpret the laws of Torah and how we make these laws meaningful in our own lives.

Some say that this Torah portion is a let-down compared to the fire and brimstone associated with the previous portion which recounted the dramatic giving of the Commandments at Mt. Sinai. Receiving the law at Mt. Sinai was meant to be a wake-up call in the most positive way. The Jews were able to reinvigorate and recharge themselves. They were able to re-Jew-venate! It was God's way of getting their attention. Sometimes we all need a boost like attending a stimulating conference or hearing an inspiring speaker to give us the motivation we need to create, share and make a difference. Sometimes, we receive negative wake-up calls in the form of an illness or upset in our lives in order to get our attention. Often, in our very busy lives, it takes a dramatic event to get our attention. We have to be shaken-up, stimulated or even brought to our knees before we take the time to stop and evaluate where we are in life and how we will move forward. But whether positive or negative, we can learn from each experience. We can take this new knowledge and use it to make informed and educated choices about how to live our lives.

Just like our ancestors who accepted the laws of God without even knowing what they were…we too accept life's blessings and life's struggles. We deal with them in our own way guided by our laws, our own inner conscience and faith. And we never have to celebrate or mourn alone. We are, as the people of Israel were at Mt. Sinai, a community, supporting each other in times of happiness and sadness. We are all part of a larger whole and we must all work together using the guidance provided to us in the Torah to lead spiritual, fulfilling and righteous lives. Amen.

NASO (OFFERINGS AND BLESSINGS)

On the Sabbath immediately following the festival of *Shavuot* we read from the Torah portion known as *Naso* (which means to "lift up"). *Naso* is the longest portion in the Torah containing one hundred and seventy-six verses. Interestingly enough, the longest tractate of the Talmud (*Bava Basra*) has one hundred and seventy-six pages, and the longest Psalm (Psalm 119) has one hundred and seventy-six verses. (I will have to explore that more at another time). *Naso* was also my Torah portion when I became a Bat Mitzvah at the age of 43.

There are two separate things that stand out to me about this portion. One of them is the extensive amount of text used to describe the gift offerings that each tribe brought for the dedication of the *Mishkan*. We learn that each and every tribe brought the same exact items for their offering, yet the portion details each of these offerings one at a time giving them each their own singular significance.

Why does the Torah take so much time to describe each of these gift offerings individually when they were all the same? Wouldn't it have been easier and briefer to list the names of the tribes and say they all brought the same gift offering each one on their own day?

Like everything in the Torah, there is a reason why the offering of each tribe is detailed separately and repeated twelve times in this portion. This is the reason we study Torah to ponder and try to answer these "why" questions. I think this part of the portion shows us that, in the eyes of God, we (just like the twelve tribes) each have individual significance. Each and every person is worthy of being seen, being heard and being acknowledged. Therefore, this teaches us an important lesson – that we should treat each person as significant giving them our time and respect and letting them know that their contributions are important.

And somewhere in the middle of this long Torah portion, we find the well-known verses that have come to be known to us as "the priestly blessing." (Numbers 6:24-26)

In the days of the Holy Temple in Jerusalem, the *Kohanim* (high priests) were tasked with being "ambassadors of God to connect and bring heaven down to earth." They bestowed this priestly blessing from God upon the people daily. Today, our rabbis often bestow this blessing at special times. The first line consists of three Hebrew words – *Y'varechecha Adonai v'yishm'recha* – May Adonai bless you and keep (or protect) you. The second line contains two additional Hebrew words (for a total of five words), but still features Adonai as the second word. – *Yisa Adonai panav elecha v'chuneka* – May Adonai deal kindly and graciously with you. The third and last line of the blessing contains seven Hebrew words and retains the word Adonai as the second word – *Yisa Adonai panav elecha v'yasem l'cha shalom* - May Adonai bestow favor upon you and grant you peace.

As the daughter of a *Kohen* and a soon to be Rabbi, I would like to offer a contemporary musical version of this blessing to each of you: ♪♪

יְבָרֶכְךָ יְהוָה וְיִשְׁמְרֶךָ:
יָאֵר יְהוָה פָּנָיו אֵלֶיךָ וִיחֻנֶּךָּ:
יִשָּׂא יְהוָה פָּנָיו אֵלֶיךָ
וְיָשֵׂם לְךָ שָׁלוֹם:

May Adonai bless and keep you. May God's countenance shine upon you. May Adonai bless you with peace. Amen

Music by: Steve Dropkin

NOACH (RAINBOWS)

I love Rainbows! For over 30 years now, a rainbow has been part of my professional logo as a family musician and the first song I ever composed was titled Keshet (Rainbow). ♪♪

Keshet, Keshet I like to see you
Up in the sky so pretty
You hide your face till after it rains
Then paint the sky with your colors
Keshet, Keshet, purple and pink
Red, yellow, blue and orange
Keshet, Keshet, I'd like to see you
Up in the sky more often.

It is a fact that rainbows are beautiful. Rainbows offer us a visual image of how awesome and mysterious nature can be. Rainbows often come after bad storms and so they have come to symbolize hope and renewed faith. Rainbows also symbolize diversity, inclusion and unity. And rainbows do not usually stick around for very long. This makes the sight of one even more special. You cannot help but feel uplifted and joyful when you witness a rainbow first hand and it is difficult not to feel awe and joy when you see a picture of a rainbow.

In our Torah portion this week, God sends a "bow in the clouds" and tells Noah that this bow in the clouds is a "sign of the covenant between Me and the earth that the waters shall never again become a flood to destroy all flesh." This rainbow is a sign from Adonai that our world will never again be destroyed as it was in the story of Noah. Our Torah commentaries tell us that the rainbow is a sign of peace in at least three different ways:

1) The rainbow represents an inverted bow – a weapon turned away so that it is not a threat.
2) The rainbow represents all colors and shades joined together to form a whole calling on all races and all types of people to do the same.
3) The rainbow represents the promise that "no matter how hard it rains, the rain will eventually stop and the sun will come out again."

For all of these reasons and more, a rainbow is special. It is a covenant between us and God. This is why we recite a special blessing whenever we see a rainbow.

בָּרוּךְ אַתָּה ה' אֱלוֹהֵינוּ מֶלֶךְ הָעוֹלָם זוֹכֵר הַבְּרִית וְנֶאֱמָן בִּבְרִיתוֹ וְקַיָם בְּמַאֲמָרוֹ

Baruch Ata Adonai Eloheynu Melech ha-olam zocher ha-b'rit v'ne-e-man biv-ri-to v'kayam b'ma-amaro.

Praised are You, Adonai, our God, King of the Universe, who remembers the covenant and is faithful to His covenant and who keeps His word.

May we continue to see rainbows in our lives and may this remarkable and beautiful sight remind us of the awesomeness of nature and our creator. May the rainbow remind us to work for peace in our world so that all people, all races, all colors, all faiths will one day realize that we are not so different and that we can all come together adding each of our parts to the rainbow of our world. Amen.

PESACH (THE NUMBER FOUR)

At the end of this month, we will celebrate Passover (*Pesach*) in our homes. This year, the first seder is on the evening of March 25th. (On Monday evening we will celebrate Passover (*Pesach*) in our homes). Passover celebrates the liberation of the Jews from slavery in Egypt and the *Haggadah* tells the story. Jewish people have always had a fascination with numbers – the number 18 stands for *chai* or life, the Jewish people wandered for 40 years in the desert, we light 8 candles on Chanukah, etc. So, it is no different with Passover. In the *Haggadah*, the number "4" is very significant. There are 4 specific instances in the *Haggadah* where the number 4 is prominent:

4 cups of wine	4 questions
4 sons	4 mentions of redemption

There are traditionally 4 cups of wine consumed as part of our Passover *seder*. The first cup of wine accompanies Kiddush and serves to sanctify the holiday. The second cup of wine is the cup of redemption because it is drunk after the telling of the Passover story when the Jews were redeemed from slavery in Egypt. The third cup of wine is drunk after the *birkat hamazon*, the blessing after the meal. It represents gratitude to God who sustains us. And, the fourth cup of wine is symbolic of the future. It is drunk near the conclusion of the *seder* when we pray for an age of peace for all humankind.

The four questions are typically recited at the *seder* table by the youngest person who is able to recite them. The answers all have to do with our unique history of slavery and redemption of the body and the soul. On *Pesach* we enjoy special freedoms that we did not enjoy when we were slaves. And it is our obligation to teach our children about Jewish customs and rituals.

There are four sons – the wise son, the wicked son, the simple son and the son who does not know enough to ask. The wise son is eager to learn. He embraces his Jewish heritage and tries to lead a righteous life. The wise son will insure the perpetuation of future

Jewish generations. The wicked son sees the requirements in the Torah as constraints on his freedom. If future Jewish generations must rely on him, there will be nothing that separates us as Jews from anyone else. The simple son has the capacity to learn, but he is lazy. He wants everything to be immediate and does not want to spend time learning or understanding about his Jewish heritage. He needs to understand that learning does not come all at once. Learning is an on-going process we continue throughout our lives. And the son who does not know enough to ask relies on each and every Jewish person to teach him the ways of Judaism to insure that he and his future generations will be Jewish.

There are four mentions of redemption in the story of the Exodus. The first, "I am Adonai and **I shall take you out** from under the burdens of Egypt" tells how Adonai showed the Egyptians that our God is a mighty God. The second, "**I shall save you** from their service" tells how Adonai brought the plagues upon the Egyptians and led the Jewish people out from slavery. The third, "**I shall redeem you** with an outstretched arm and with great punishments" tells of the miraculous parting of the Red Sea where the Jewish people crossed on dry land while the sea swallowed up the pursuing Egyptians. And the fourth, "**I shall take you** to me as a People, and I shall be a G-d to you" tells of the spiritual redemption of the Jewish people to become a holy nation.

There are also four seasons. Passover comes at the true beginning of the Jewish year – the springtime - a time of rebirth and renewal for our world just as it was for the Jewish slaves who left Egypt to become a new Jewish nation. There are four matriarchs – Sarah, Rebecca, Rachel and Leah – the mothers of our Jewish people.

No one really knows what the connection to the number 4 is with Passover, but all of these symbolisms of 4 give us something to think about as we celebrate this Passover of renewal of nature, renewal of spirit and hopefully, like the wise son, a desire for learning throughout our lives.

May each and every one of you have a happy and meaningful Passover. Amen.

ROSH HASHANAH
(DESTROY, DEFINE OR DEVELOP)

I read something on the internet that just made a light bulb go off in my head as I was thinking about the High Holy Days and the *D'var* I needed to write for class this week. The quote read:

"You have three choices when bad things happen to you: You can let it <u>destroy</u> you, you can let it <u>define</u> you, or you can let it <u>develop</u> you."

I thought of this quote in the context of Abraham, sometimes called the Father of Judaism. One of the portions that we read on Rosh Hashanah is *Akedat Yitzchak* or the "binding of Isaac." When Abraham was ordered to sacrifice his son (his seed) Isaac, this was the ultimate test of faith between Abraham and Adonai. This was a very bad thing that was happening to Abraham and his family.

However, Abraham was not willing to let this test of faith DESTROY him. He held on to his unending faith in Adonai and ultimately his son, Isaac, was spared.

Abraham also did not let this bad episode in his life DEFINE him. Abraham is known for so much more than just his willingness to sacrifice his beloved son.

But Abraham did allow this event to DEVELOP him. He was able to learn through this experience that our God is a loving God. That God rewards those who are faithful and follow the commandments. Abraham not only learned and developed from this experience, but he went on to share his beliefs with many others resulting in the belief in one God that Jews have today.

May we all learn from Abraham's example and not allow tragedy and negativity to define or destroy us. But, instead, allow ourselves to learn and grow from each experience in life – both the good and the bad. May we all be sealed for another year of blessing and health in the Book of Life. *Shanah Tovah*.

SHABBAT

The celebration of Shabbat is one of the most basic ways that we can "be Jewish" on a weekly basis. In our Torah, we are commanded numerous times to cease from work and instead, to rest on Shabbat. Shabbat is given special status as a holy day at the very beginning of the Torah in Genesis, Chapter 2. And later in Exodus, Chapter 20, it is our 4th commandment – "Remember the Sabbath Day and keep it holy."

In our community of Reform Jews, most of us do not distinguish between our work week and Shabbat, the day of rest. Observant Jews take much of the Torah literally and follow the laws for cessation from work and practice the rituals associated with the celebration of Shabbat. For those of us who attend Shabbat services, this should be a time when we can slow down, take time to breathe and think about the abundance and beauty that surrounds us. Shabbat offers us a time of reflection, renewal and rest. We are talking about approximately 24 hours out of each week. Twenty four hours where we can choose to slow down, stop working, reflect on the past week, renew, recharge and rest. Is this asking too much? I think not.

The key word here is "choose". We, as Jews, must choose to be Jewish. We must choose to keep Shabbat and other Jewish rituals so that our children and our children's children will still be Jewish. It is important to be a part of a Jewish community, to celebrate holidays and special occasions together. On Shabbat, we can choose to make a conscious effort to be Jewish. Here are a few things to try:

1) Attend a Shabbat service to be a part of a community.
2) Prepare a special Shabbat meal with a beautifully set table.
3) Light the Shabbat candles, say *Kiddush* and *motzi*.
4) Reflect on all you have to be thankful for. Create a family prayer.
5) Ask each member of your family to describe one good thing they did during the previous week; or say one thing they are thankful for.

6) Remember the three commandments of Shabbat: holiness (*kedushah*); rest (*menucha*); and joy (*oneg*). What can you do on Shabbat to connect to each of these?
7) Set aside some time on Shabbat to do something special that you normally do not do: take a walk, take a nap, spend family time together, read.
8) Make *Havdalah* on Saturday evening to say goodbye to Shabbat.
9) Use greetings like "*Shabbat Shalom*" to welcome Shabbat and "*Shavua Tov*" to welcome the new week.
10) Sing some Shabbat songs or listen to recordings of Shabbat music.

I urge you to try some of these simple things to make Shabbat special in your life as a Jew. You don't have to do them all at once. But, hopefully, as you add each one (in no particular order), you will continue to see how much the observance of Shabbat can enrich your life. Rituals like these are special. They give order and meaning to our lives. They make us Jewish. Amen.

SHABBAT SHIRA

♪ ♪ Begin with singing Sufi *Hallelu*….. (expressing joy)

This Shabbat is perhaps one of my favorites. The obvious reason is because I am a singer and it is Shabbat Shira…the Sabbath of Song! I cannot imagine a world – or even a day - without music. Music is so powerful and truly a universal language with the ability to **express ecstatic joy and praise, break down barriers of communication, soothe and heal.**

The Torah portion this week features the miraculous crossing of the Red Sea as the Jewish people leave slavery in Egypt for a journey to a new land of promise. The Egyptians follow and the Jewish people watch as the Red Sea swallows them up. In celebration of this miracle, Moses leads the people in a song of praise to God, while Miriam, his sister, "takes her timbrel in her hand" and leads the women in song and dance. In this week's

Haftarah, Devorah, the judge and prophetess, rallies the Jewish people to fight and win a battle against the Canaanites. After the victory, like Moses and Miriam, she leads the Jewish people in a song of praise to God. Moses, Miriam and Devorah all used music to express ecstatic praise and joy.

One of my favorite quotes is: "When you sing, you pray twice". The quote is attributed to St. Augustine, a 5th century African bishop. Singing or chanting has always been an important part of our Jewish tradition. In many religions, including our own, the first forms of prayer were chanting and song. In the late 19th and early 20th centuries, the *hazzan* or cantor (and a kosher butcher) were often the first professional people hired by a Jewish community even before hiring a rabbi. It was felt that the *hazzan* (and the butcher) provided a more immediate need.

Another favorite quote is one by E.T.A. Hoffman (who wrote the novella on which the Nutcracker ballet is based) – "Where language stops, music begins." It is true that music transcends all barriers. When people cannot communicate, because of differences in language, culture, and opinions, music quickly becomes a commonality. And music is used very prominently in working with autistic children and those recovering from traumatic head injuries and stroke. Sometimes music is the miracle that breaks down barriers and facilitates better communication.

OD YAVO SHALOM ALEINU ♪♪	PEACE WILL COME TO US
(SALAAM)	
Od yavo' shalom aleinu	Peace will come upon us
Od yavo' shalom aleinu	Peace will come upon us
Od yavo' shalom aleinu	Peace will come upon us
Ve al kulam (x2)	and on everyone.
Salaam (Salaam)	Salaam *('peace' in Arabic)*
Aleinu ve al kol ha olam,	On us and on everyone
Salaam, Salaam (x2)	Salaam, Salaam

Ten years ago, I founded a non-profit organization called Arts and Healthcare (www.artsandhealthcare.org). Our mission is to bring innovative arts experiences into healthcare settings to assist with the healing process. In my work with this organization, I have often had the opportunity and privilege to sing at the bedside of seriously ill or injured patients. Most are unconscious and hooked up to ventilators. I have witnessed over and over again, the power that music has to help many of these patients recover. It is amazing to see how bodies that were agitated, calm down, limbs that were twisted, untwist and breathing that was labored and erratic, becomes even.

In almost every ancient culture, music was used as a major source of healing. Our own history can claim King David as the very first Jewish music therapist. Throughout the Bible, we learn that he was an accomplished musician with the ability to soothe and comfort by playing his harp or lyre. He also wrote most of our *Tehillim* or Psalms, many of which were specifically written to comfort and heal.

In the current Reform Jewish culture, prayers for healing have become greatly significant. Healing circles are now commonplace and the *Misheberach* prayer has become a centerpiece of many Reform worship services. When leading the *Misheberach* prayer, I always ask that we remember those among us who need healing – healing of mind, healing of body…healing of spirit. And that we should include ourselves in these prayers as each and every one of us needs peace and healing every day.

♪ ♪ *Mi shebeirach avoteinu mekor habracha l'imoteinu*

May the Source of strength
Who blessed the ones before us
Help us find the courage
To make our lives a blessing,
And let us say: Amen.

Mi shebeirach imoteinu mekor habracha l'avoteinu
Bless those in need of healing With *refuah shleima*:
The renewal of body,
The renewal of spirit,
And let us say: Amen

Music is very powerful. It can raise us up to joy and ecstasy. It can break down cultural barriers and it can bring peace and healing. I leave you with one final quote (that I have modified a bit) by the Jewish poet, Berthold Auerbach ~ "Music [like Shabbat] washes away from the soul the dust of everyday life." Amen & Good Shabbos.

SHELACH L'CHA (TALLITOT)

This week, we read from *Shelach L'cha*, the 37th weekly Torah portion found in the book of Numbers. *Shelach L'cha* is often translated to mean "send for yourself" and refers to God's command to Moses to send spies, one from each tribe, to scout out the land of Israel. Much of the portion deals with this expedition to the Promised Land and the report of the spies as to what they found and their recommendations. However, the most interesting part of this portion for me was the very last paragraph, Numbers Chapter 15, verses 37-41.

In these few verses, Adonai tells Moses to instruct the Israelites to "make for themselves *tzitzit* (or fringes) on the corners of their garments throughout the ages." The command goes on to say: "Let them attach a cord of blue to the fringe at each corner. That shall be your fringe; look at it and recall all the commandments of the Lord and observe them."

These five verses make up the 3rd block of text in the *K'riat Shema* (along with Deuteronomy Chapter 6, verses 4-9 [what we know as the *Shema* & *V'ahavta*] and Deuteronomy Chapter 11, verses 13-21 [usually deleted from Reform ritual]). This complete prayer is recited by traditional Jews each day in the morning and in the evening.

There is a joke about a man named Shlomie. Who brings his *tallit* to the dry cleaners to be cleaned. When he picks it up, he is stunned to see a bill for $105 dollars. "Why so much?" Shlomie asks. The dry cleaner explains, "Five dollars to clean the garment, and 100 dollars to get out all those knots!" The verses we read this Shabbat from Numbers, Chapter 15 tell us just how important the fringes and knots are.

As a Reform Jewish woman, I have not worn a *tallit* for that long and in my home congregation, I am the only woman who does. However, I feel a sense of comfort and belonging when I wear a *tallit*. Somehow, I just feel more holy.

Rashi provides some very interesting commentary on the tallit and specifically the fringes. Rashi makes a comparison with the spies in the beginning of this portion. He shares that the heart and the eyes are spies for the body, and they act as the body's agents. The eyes see, the heart desires and the body carries out the action. We have a choice to make the action holy or unholy. The fringes are found on all four sides of a *tallit*. They are a visual reminder of God's presence everywhere.

We are commanded by God to look at the fringes with our eyes. And these fringes, much like a string we tie around our finger, will remind us to remember and observe all of God's commandments throughout each generation. The numerical value of the Hebrew word "*tzitzit*" is 600. There are 8 strings and 5 knots on each fringe. If you add all this up, it equals 613…the total number of commandments we are to observe. Coincidence? I think not.

The portion also mentions a blue *techelet* thread which was to be found wrapped in each fringe. During the destruction of the Temple and the exile of the Jews to Babylon, the dye for this blue thread became almost impossible to find and so most tallit do not contain this special *techelet* thread. However, in 1993, a non-profit organization named *P'til Techelet* (*techelet* thread) was founded with the sole purpose of returning this ancient custom to the Jewish people. The dye for the blue thread comes from a rare snail called the *murex trunculus* and is the same color as the garments worn by the high priests and found in the tapestries in the Tabernacle. This blue is the color of the sea. The sea is a reflection of the color of the heavens, the seat of God's glory. It reminds us of our closeness to Adonai. Especially when we wrap ourselves in the *tallit*, we should feel closer to God, closer to our heritage and closer to the generations that came before us and those yet to come. Amen.

SHEMINI (FAITH)

This week's Torah portion, *Shemini* (which means eighth) begins with Moses commanding Aaron to make a purification offering to God. This offering occurs on the eighth day after Aaron and his sons have gone through 7 days of ordination and preparation as *Kohanim* or priests of the Tabernacle. Shortly thereafter, two of Aaron's sons are consumed by fire and killed as they make their offering to Adonai. The Torah portion is not very clear about the reasons for their death and there exists much commentary about this. Some say that they made an offering that was not asked for – that they were too eager and God did not need their help. Others say they were too eager in another way by bearing the fire of ambition hoping that their elders would die so that they could take over. Still others say that they came too close to God motivated by excessive devotion. But most of the commentaries state that they did not have enough respect for their position or God and arrived at the sanctuary in a drunken state.

In fact, in the next part of the Torah portion, God speaks directly to Aaron for the first time saying to him: ***"Yayin veshechar al-tesht atah"*** - You shall not drink strong wine to the point of intoxication. God goes on to tell Aaron that as a priest and leader of the people, he is responsible for distinguishing between the sacred and profane, the pure and impure and that it is up to Aaron to teach the Israelites all the laws imparted to them through Moses.

Obviously, if God chooses to speak directly to Aaron for the first time, this is an important moment. Is it out of compassion that God chooses to speak to Aaron in this special way? And what should we make of God's command to Aaron to not be intoxicated?

Aaron has just lost two of his sons. And after this loss, instead of weeping or condemning, Aaron is silent. Some commentaries say that Aaron was the consummate priest. That although he was weeping on the inside, he was able to keep it together on the outside. He was able to be silent and take time to try to understand the deeper meaning of what had happened. Even though something horrible had happened to him personally, he was still able to love and have faith in God. Those who serve God have abundant faith and their faith helps them to unlock and share the secrets of God's love for us. Through his silence, Aaron was able to see the full picture. God speaks directly to Aaron because he has proven himself as a true and faithful leader…one who will serve God and one who can be trusted with the mysteries of our faith. God talks to Aaron about not becoming intoxicated because our Jewish faith tells us that we do not need external temptations or escapes to help us find inner peace and prayer. The messages of the Torah are to be found right here on earth with our feet planted firmly on the ground. By stating that we should not enter into prayer while intoxicated, God is telling us that we will not find God through some sort of out of body experience or numbing of our senses, but instead through sober study and the performance of *mitzvot* with a clear mind and faithful intention.

When bad things happen, it is often difficult to have faith. And some turn to harmful escapes like drugs or alcohol in order to cope. But we must all use Aaron as a positive example of how to be strong, how to be silent and stoic in the face of adversity. We must try to "step away" and see the bigger picture of what God has in store for us. Like Aaron, in the silence we pray to find meaning and the hope to go on with faith in Adonai. Amen.

SIMCHAT TORAH

♪♪ To everything, turn, turn, turn

    There is a season, turn, turn, turn
    And a time to every purpose under heaven
    A time to be born – a time to die
    A time to plant – a time to reap
    A time to kill – a time to heal
    A time to laugh – a time to weep

As the words of this song from Ecclesiastes (made popular by The Byrds) implies, our lives are all about turning and opposites, looking at things in new ways and making choices. During the High Holy Days, we turn and <u>re</u>turn promising to do better in the year ahead. Each and every day, we have the opportunity to make choices. We can choose between good and evil, right and wrong, blessing and curse. On *Simchat Torah* we literally turn our sacred Torah back to the beginning starting our annual readings all over again. We read from the very end of Deuteronomy about the death and legacy of Moses and then we return to the beginning of the Torah and read from the first chapter of Genesis describing the story of God's creation of the world.

Beginnings and endings….endings and beginnings. Our Torah never stops. It offers us a never ending cycle of learning, questioning, commenting and seeing our history with fresh eyes. Even our actions on *Simchat Torah* mirror this never ending cycle as we process around the synagogue joyfully with the Torah for our *hakafot*.

Rabbi Ben Bag Bag, a 1st century rabbi taught, "Turn the Torah and turn it again, for everything you want to know can be found within it." Each year when we read from our sacred Torah, we are able to look at it with fresh eyes always interpreting and seeing new meanings and messages. We must always turn and <u>re</u>turn again and again as we study and question, learn and grow, share and confirm. Only then can we try to understand that there is a season and a time to every purpose under heaven.

♪♪ To everything, turn, turn, turn

There is a season, turn, turn, turn
And a time to every purpose under heaven. Amen.

SPELLING BEE (K-N-A-I-D-E-L)

On Thursday, May 30th, 2013, the 86th Annual Scripps National Spelling Bee was held in Oxen Hill, Maryland, a suburb of the District of Columbia. There were initially 281 contestants between the ages of 8 and 14 who competed in Maryland for the $30,000 prize and trophy. On Thursday, at exactly 8:05 am, the eleven finalists were introduced: 3 from Florida; 2 from New York; 2 from Texas; and individual contestants from Illinois, Kansas, Utah and Massachusetts. The South was not represented at all.

Here are some little known facts about the Spelling Bee:

1) There is a secret committee that comes up with the word list. No one knows who is on this committee. It is top secret.

2) A word gets selected to be on the list because it is not transparent. So, you hear lots of words that are double letters (*braggadocio*), single letters where you might expect double letters (*sassafras*), silent letters (*mnemonic*), and letter combinations that most of us never encounter.

3) A speller's most dangerous foe is the schwa – it can be represented as any vowel (as in *America*, *history*, or *belief* and can even be silent, in words like *rhyth(ə)m*)

4) A majority of the contestants go on to become doctors and scientists rather than wordsmiths in the media or academia. Perhaps unsurprisingly, this year's group of spellers most frequently cited math as their favorite subject. It seems that

there is something about the kind of brain that is not intimidated by the dictionary in childhood that seems well-suited to the work of medicine in adulthood.

One by one, the eleven finalists are eliminated on words such as *pathognomonic* (path-o-no-mo-nic), *melocoton* (may-lo-co-TONE), *cipollino* (Sip-ah-lee-no), and many other words so daunting, I won't even attempt to pronounce them.

By 9:54 am, the field of spellers is down to just two young men - Pranav Sivakumar (a 13 year old from Illinois) and Arvind Mahankali (nicknamed "Smoking Jacket" because he gave an interview wearing a red satin smoking jacket). By 10:22 am, the judges are down to the sheet containing the 25 final words. If both contestants spell all of them correctly, they become co-champions. After a few words, Pranav misses on a word I can't even pronounce. Arvind must spell two words in a row correctly in order to be declared the champion. He spells the first word – *tokonoma* (a Japanese word meaning a niche in a wall that is spelled just like it sounds). Then the final word – *knaidel*. The 13 year old from Bayside Hills, NY has won -- spelling a German/Yiddish word! A matzo ball wins the spelling bee!! Now, we as Jews know that there can be various spellings for the word *knaidel*. He won by spelling it K-N-A-I-D-E-L. But would he have also won if had spelled it K-N-E-I-D-E-L or K-N-E-Y-D-L? It is sort of like the words *Dreydl* or *Chanukah*. There are variations in spelling. In any event, the young 13 year old, who has never eaten a *knaidel*, has just elevated Yiddish to a cool place in American pop culture. Thanks, Arvind and enjoy your first *knaidel*. Amen.

TAZRIA – METZORA (BALANCE)

This Shabbat, we arrive at perhaps the two most dreaded Torah portions of all. *Tazria*, meaning she conceives and *Metzora*, a person afflicted with a terrible skin disease. In leap years (2014 will be a leap year), *Tazria* is read separately. In common years (which include 2013 and 2015), *Tazria* is combined with the next Torah portion, *Metzora*, to help achieve the number of weekly readings needed to read the entire Torah in the cycle of a year. So, in this current year, the two portions are combined. These two Torah portions talk about things that no *B'nai Mitzvah* wishes to share especially at the tender age of 13. The portions speak of "*tzara'at*" – an affliction similar to leprosy. They also talk about childbirth, sexual diseases and the impurity of women at certain times of the month. Certainly not the most sought after Torah portions.

However, these portions do have some important lessons to teach us even today. We are told that someone who has *tzara'at* is called a *metzora* – thus the name of one of the Torah portions. When it is determined that the *metzora* is cured of his affliction, he must be purified by the *Kohanim* before he can return to society. In order to be purified, the person is required to bring two live kosher birds, a piece of cedar, some crimson wool and hyssop (a type of grass). The rabbis tell us that the disease of *tzara'at* is brought on by the sin of haughtiness, arrogance or *lashon hara* – speaking evil about another. Each of these items needed for purification relates to this sin in some way.

The commentaries help explain these purification items and their significance to this sin. The piece of cedar is brought because it comes from a tree of great height and stature. This represents the haughtiness and presumed superiority of the afflicted person. The crimson wool and the hyssop are considered very lowly. The dye for the crimson wool was taken from the eggs of an insect and the hyssop is one of the smallest of all growing things. They show the afflicted person that, in order to achieve forgiveness, he must strive to become more like them – humble and modest. Two live kosher birds are brought as well. These two birds who chatter with one another, symbolize the gossip and slander that the afflicted person spoke. The *Kohen* slaughters one of the birds and pours its blood into an earthen vessel. The blood shows that by speaking evil, a person causes pain and suffering to another. This sends a very powerful message to the wrongdoer – when someone speaks evil of another, he cuts himself off from society. And, this afflicted person has spent much time in isolation before the *Kohanim* determine that he is ready for the purification rites. This is why the second bird is set free to fly among the other birds. The release and free flight of this bird shows that, even though someone has committed a wrong, their life can and must go on. It is balance, not withdrawal, that we must find. We must think before we speak. We must consider the feelings of our fellow man. We must walk humbly with our God. Amen.

TERUMAH (A HOLY PLACE)

Terumah is the name of this week's Torah portion. There are several different translations of this word from Hebrew to English. One of the most common translations is that *Terumah* means "donation" or "offering". But if you take the literal meaning, the word *Terumah* means "lifting up", or "to elevate". In the Torah portion, it referred to the physical act of lifting up to the altar what was being offered to God. But, according to many modern commentaries, it can also mean that the act of giving to God and your religious community elevates the giver to a higher level. The Torah portion begins with God telling Moses to "Tell the Israelite people to bring Me gifts; you shall accept gifts for Me from every person whose heart so moves him." We should give because we want to – because our heart moves us to do so. And when we give, we feel good – it is as simple as that.

Because I run a non-profit organization, I often ask people for money to help us continue to do our good work in the community. The standard thing I say when people ask how much they should give is to "give until you feel good, not until it hurts." This provides a great measuring stick for how to give. You also can only give what you are capable of giving. It may not always be money, but it may be your time or your talent or physical objects. So, the question is, does God really need our gifts? Did God really need gifts from the Israelites in the desert? Doesn't God have everything?

In the portion, God not only asked for gifts given from the heart, but also asks the Jewish people to "make Me a sanctuary that I may dwell among [you]." And then God gives the Jewish people very specific details of how this sanctuary (or *Mishkan*) should be constructed. This *Mishkan* was made to order by the Israelites and it sat in the center of their camp in the desert. The *Mishkan* was designed so that it could be transported from place to place as the Jewish people wandered in the desert. Once the Jewish people reached the Promised Land of Israel, a larger more permanent version of the *Mishkan* was constructed on the Temple Mount in Jerusalem. And today, there are many sanctuaries throughout the world where Jews worship, study and congregate. Since those instructions given by God in this Torah portion, God has had a sanctuary on earth in which to dwell among us.

But, again, we ask the question, "why does God need our gifts? Why did God need for us to build him a sanctuary or a home?" There is a wonderful midrash that tells of a king who had only one daughter. One day she married a prince from another country and he wanted to return to his country with his new bride. The father stopped him and said, "My daughter is my only child and I cannot part with her. But she is also your wife and I cannot tell you not to take her." So the father asked for one favor: "wherever you go to live, prepare a room for me so that I may dwell with you for I cannot leave my daughter." In this same way, God said to the Jewish people: "I have given you the Torah. I cannot part with her and I also cannot tell you where to take her. But, wherever you go, make for Me a house where I may dwell."

This is a beautiful analogy of how each of us can bring God into our lives. We take pride in our own homes. We decorate them, make them comfortable and safe. A sanctuary, like a home, should be beautiful, comfortable and safe. The sanctuary is a physical example of God's home on earth. Even today, our sanctuaries have similar objects in them as those specified by God to be in the *Mishkan* – the *aron ha-kodesh*, the *bimah*, the *menorah*.

God gave the Jewish people the tools and instructions with which to build the sanctuary. And each and every person contributed to the creation of the *Mishkan* through physical labor and contributions or "*terumah*". Even today, the building and maintaining of a synagogue rests collectively on all of its members. It is up to each and every one of us to give until it feels good and to give what we uniquely have to give in order to make God's home among us comfortable, beautiful and safe.

♪♪ These are the gifts that we bring that we may build a holy place

>This is the spirit that we bring that we may build a holy place
>We will bring all the goodness that comes from our hearts
>And the spirit of God will dwell within. Amen.

TETZAVEH (THE CLOTHES MAKE THE MAN)

I come from a long line of clothing retailers and I was even trained in retail marketing and management myself. My great-grandfather, David Caplan, arrived in America around 1888 as a young boy of 16. He was from the small Polish town of Naravke and was sponsored to come over to America by Mr. Bernard Ginsberg, a man from his home town in Poland. Mr. Ginsberg (no relation to my husband) had opened a dry goods store in Central Louisiana and was looking for young boys to peddle goods from his store to other places in the state. For several years, my great-grandfather peddled clothing and other necessities and in 1891, he decided to open his own dry goods store on Front Street in downtown Alexandria, Louisiana. Clothing was always a staple item in the store – in particular clothing for men. During the war years, the store catered primarily to the military providing uniforms and clothing for our soldiers. My grandfather and grandmother, Abe and Jeannice Caplan worked in the store for many of these war years. It was around this time that the store began selling not only uniforms but men's working clothes as well. In the 1950's my father, Edwin Caplan, the oldest of their three boys, came into the business after graduating at the top of his class at Tulane

University where he met my mother. It was at this time, that our store became a men's specialty shop and expanded to several other locations including a store at the very first strip mall in town and a store at the very first enclosed shopping mall in town. My dad retired from the business about 15 years ago and the one remaining store – still in downtown Alexandria – is now run by my uncle, aunt and cousin. The current store primarily sells uniforms now catering to law enforcement, schools and corporations.

So now that you know a little bit about my retail heritage, you will easily see why I was drawn to the part of this portion that goes into great detail about the clothing – or "uniforms" that Aaron and the other high priests (*Kohanim*) were instructed to wear. This Torah portion devotes more than 40 verses to the topic of the clothing worn by the high priests and how these garments are to be made. Nowhere else in the Torah is clothing described in such detail.

As they say, "the clothes make the man" and "you are what you wear". When Aaron and the high priests engaged in work that was holy, they needed to be suitably dressed in holy garments. These were clothes that added *kavod* (glory) and *tiferet* (splendor) to their work. According to Ramban (Rabbi Moses ben Nachman) the command to dress the high priests in garments for glory and splendor is not only to enhance the status of the priest himself, but also to enhance the glory of God. Ramban continues by noting that *kavod* and *tiferet* are *sefirot*, a *Kabbilistic* term for emanations of God. So, through these very specific types of clothing worn by the priests or *Kohanim*, God is connecting with the people. The spark of God that resides in all of us is brought out in the priests and worn on the outside with his clothing. What we wear and how we dress is a constant reminder of who we are and our relationship with Adonai. By wearing these holy garments, Aaron and the other *Kohanim* were constantly reminded of their special role. When a king wears a crown and robes, he commands respect and honor. When we wear a *kippah* or *tallit*, we show respect to our Jewish heritage and to Adonai. When we dress up, we feel special. As Jews, we also make our traditions special. On Shabbat, we dress up our table with a beautiful tablecloth, polished candlesticks and a silver Kiddush cup. Would Shabbat be as special if we used an ordinary table cloth and drank wine from a paper cup?

Clothing and adornments DO make a difference. This is why many Jews choose to wear a *kippah* in the sanctuary and wear a *tallit* when the Torah is read. This is why we bring out our best china for Pesach and set a beautiful table for Shabbat. Just like the priests, by making our clothing and adornments special, we are constantly reminded of our special role as Jews. By adding beauty, we add to the holiness of the act. We all have the potential to be holy, perhaps we just need to dress the part. Amen.

THANKSGIVUKKAH 2013

Since our topic of study this week was Chanukah, I decided to write about the most unusual occurrence of the first day of Chanukah falling on Thanksgiving for the first time ever this year. Brilliant physicists have calculated that this will not happen again for over 70,000 years! How lucky are we to be able to celebrate this momentous occasion!

When our children were growing up, we always tried to make Chanukah fun. Our dining room would be turned into a Chanukah room with decorations, menorahs and gifts galore. We even had a tradition for many years of a Chanukah Balloon…a gigantic balloon that you could put a few small gifts in and lots of confetti. This was always the centerpiece at the Chanukah table. And, on the last night of Chanukah, our children would thrill in being able to pop the Chanukah balloon to retrieve their gifts. The confetti would fly – and I would try to enjoy it for the moment not thinking about the clean up afterwards.

Well, now we have two little granddaughters and we always celebrate Chanukah at our house. There is no more Chanukah balloon, but this year, we are pulling out all the stops with Thanksgivukkah! And so are many of the Jewish merchants. There are Thanksgivukkah t-shirts (I bought one), Thanksgivukkah cards, Thanksgivukkah songs and even a Thanksgivukkah menorah called a Menurky – I ordered one of those too. Here is a taste of some of the Thanksgivukkah songs that will be sung around our Thanksgivukkah table this year:

By Hazzan Mike Stein to the tune of "Lichvod HaChanukah" ♪♪

My father gave me a turkey leg
Latkes and cranberry sauce (2x)
Oh, do you know what it is for?
Do you know what it is for?
Do you know what it is for?
It's for Thanksgivukkah!

To the tune of I Have A Little Dreydl: ♪♪

I have a little dreydl	I have a little dreydl
I made it out of clay	I made it out of turkey
And when it's dry and ready	I left it in the sun too long
It will be Thanksgiving Day.	And now it's turkey jerkey
Oh, dreydl, turkey, dreydl	Oh, dreydl, turkey, dreydl
I'll eat and then I'll play	Nun, gobble, shin and hey
Turkey and latkes	Oh, dredyl, turkey, dreydl
On Thanksgivukkah Day	It's the best Thanksgiving Day!

At this point, you may think I have totally lost my mind, but there is a reason for all this silly celebration. What a wonderful opportunity this holiday provides to teach about both Thanksgiving and Chanukah. Both holidays revolve around special foods and religious freedom. I promise you, our granddaughters will never forget their first and only Thanksgivukkah as we light the Menurkey and sing the candle blessings. And as we sing the silly songs and play dredyl. The best memories are made when things are fun and different and unique. When families come together to share something that will need to be remembered for a lifetime because it will never happen again. Amen.

V'YAKHEL PEKUDEY (CHAZAK, CHAZAK)

In this week's double Torah portion, we read from the last books of *Sh'mot* or Exodus. And whenever we come to the end of one of the books of our Torah, we traditionally say the words, "*Chazak, Chazak, V'nitchazeik*" - translated as "Be Strong, Be Strong, and we will be strengthened." Where does this custom come from and what can we learn from it?

This custom seems to have its origins in two similar occurrences involving the prophet, Joshua. The first in Deuteronomy, chapter 31, where Moses, at the end of his life, tells the Jewish people and Joshua to "be strong and of good courage." Moses first tells the Jewish people (in verse 6) that he will not lead them into the Promised Land, but that God has chosen Joshua for this task and that they all should be strong. Then (in verse 7) Moses gives these same words of advice to Joshua "in the sight of all Israel." And, finally, God speaks to Joshua for the first time (in verse 23) charging him to be strong and resolute. The second instance of this phrase appearing is in chapter 1 of the book of Joshua. When Joshua is chosen to lead the Jewish people into the Promised Land, God commands Joshua to "be strong and of good courage". This command appears three times in the first 9 verses of the book of Joshua.

With the death of Moses, the Jewish people had to feel a bit uneasy about their new leader and Joshua probably had some self-doubt as well. Whenever there is change or transition, there can be fear of the unknown and uncertainty. These commands to Joshua from both Moses and Adonai offered words of encouragement to the newly chosen leader and also comforted and strengthened the resolve of the Jewish people.

Just as the Jewish people transitioned from one leader to another, we transition from one book of the Torah to another. At the end of each book of Torah, there is white space – the unknown. And at the end of each book of Torah, we say "*Chazak, Chazak, V'nitchazeik.*" Just as these words were spoken three times in

Deuteronomy and three times in the book of Joshua, we say them three times as we transition as well.

But, I think there is more to this. We repeat the word *"chazak"* twice. When we say, *"Chazak, chazek"*, we are using the singular form of the word. We are referring to an individual. But by saying it twice, we not only include ourselves, but others as well. And the end of the phrase is *"v'nitchazeik"*, the plural form of the word indicating that individuals working together bring strength to one another. As a community, we are stronger, we have less fear and we can accomplish more.

It is said that the world depends on three things: *Torah* (prayer), *Avodah* (study) and *Gemilut Chassodim* (deeds of loving kindness). All of these things are usually done with and for others. We come together as a community to pray. And when we pray, our prayers connect us not only to Adonai, but also to our people. We learn so much more when we study with others. Our study is enriched with the insight that each person brings as we look at so many different facets of our Torah and traditions. And we could not fulfill the mitzvot of *gemilut chassodim* without others.

So, when we reach uncertain or transitional places in our own lives, just like with our Torah, we can take comfort in the fact that we are not alone. That if we are strong and if our neighbor is strong, then together, we are stronger and anything is possible. *"Chazak, Chazak, V'nitchazeik"* Be strong, be strong and may we strengthen one another. Amen.

VAYEISHEV (OUR UNIQUE GIFTS)

This week, we read from Genesis chapters 37-40 known as *Vayeishev* which means, "he settled" or lived referring to the fact that Jacob had settled in the land of Canaan, the land of his father, Isaac.

In this portion, it is made very clear that Jacob favors Joseph and

Benjamin, (his two sons born to his favorite wife, Rachel), more than the sons born to his other wives. Jacob does nothing to hide this fact and blatantly showers Joseph with praise and gifts such as the "coat of many colors" he gives to him. This favoritism pits Joseph, through no fault of his own, against his brothers and the Torah tells us that the brothers "hated him so that they could not speak a friendly word to him." To make matters worse, Joseph has dreams...dreams that make him appear to be better than his brothers. Instead of keeping these dreams to himself, Joseph haughtily shares them. This only makes him seem more superior to his brothers and makes them so jealous that they want to kill him.

For weeks now, the book of Genesis has been full of family dysfunction. Remember, Jacob grew up in a family where his mother, Rebecca favored him and his father, Isaac favored his twin brother, Esau. There was constant trickery, betrayal and jockeying for position of the most "loved." This was the example that was set for Jacob. It is easy to see how Jacob's behavior demonstrates that it is much easier to repeat known patterns, even destructive ones, than to create new ones. Bad habits are hard to break.

The Torah teaches that every person has a unique role to play in our world. I do not think it is a coincidence that this Torah portion is read on the Sabbath before Chanukah. On Chanukah, we light 8 candles in our menorah. Each candle looks the same, but each one is treated as an individual candle. Each one has their own light that shines. Some light easily and others are difficult to light. Some burn very quickly and others take a longer time to extinguish.

This is also true with our children....they may look similar and even act similarly, but each child has their own unique gifts or light to share with our world in their own way and in their own time. It is our duty as parents and teachers to discover the special light of each child, and to help each child learn how to share their talents for the betterment of our world. As one rabbi put it,

"Greatness is not determined by what gifts and talents we have, but rather by what we do with those gifts." May we learn from the mistakes of Jacob and his children to recognize our unique gifts so that we can share them with others. And may we accept our successes with humility. Amen.

VAYERA
(THERE'S ALWAYS ROOM FOR ONE MORE)

♪ "There's always room for one more, maybe two or three or four

There's always space for another face, around our Sabbath table."
(song by Fran Avni & Jackie Cytrynbaum)

At the beginning of *Parsha Vayera*, "the Lord appears to Abraham." But, when Abraham looks up, he sees three men. He runs (not walks) to eagerly greet them and insists upon bathing their feet, making them comfortable and feeding them royally. These three men, whom he has never met before, are cause for Abraham to interrupt his time with God. We understand that in the Torah portion, these three strangers are really angels or messengers from God, but Abraham is unaware of this. His actions are indicative of how he would treat any stranger approaching his home. His hospitality was genuine and honest. Abraham did not just welcome these strangers, he made them <u>feel</u> welcome.

In Hebrew, this concept of welcoming the stranger, is called *Hachnasat Orchim* and it is one of the "obligations without measure" that we recite in the *Shacharit* service. The Talmud suggests that Abraham interrupted his conversation with God to attend to the needs of his guests, thereby indicating that *Hachnasat Orchim* "is more important even than experiencing the Divine presence." This emphasizes that welcoming and caring for the stranger is one of our most important *mitzvot*.

Time and time again, we read in the Torah about how we should take care of and welcome the stranger "for you were once strangers in the land of Egypt." In fact, no other commandment is referred to as many times in the Torah as this one (36 times to be exact).

For thousands of years, Jews have taken *Hachnasat Orchim* to heart. We typically welcome strangers and those new to our community to eat at our Sabbath table, to join us under the sukkah and to experience the *Pesach seder* with us. Even Tevya, in <u>Fiddler on the Roof,</u> invited Perchick, the student, to join him and his family at their Sabbath table.

I recently became aware of an organization that is promoting the Sabbath table and the welcoming of strangers to it. It is called "Guess Who's Coming to Shabbas?"

This organization, started by a women in the Philadelphia area, encourages congregations to have their members host Shabbat meals in their homes where they welcome people in their Jewish community who may be strangers to them. These dinners are held 4-5 times a year with different hosts and a variety of guests. It is a wonderful way to create community within a congregation and to fulfill the mitzvah of *Hachnasat Orchim*. "Guess Who's Coming to Shabbas?" stresses the welcoming and the companionship of other people much more than the food or drink served. The Sabbath offers us an opportunity to stop our work and our dependency on technology and instead, to just spend time with people. I encourage you to try it. For more information on "Guess Who's Coming to Shabbas?" please visit http://guesswhoscomingtoshabbas.org/ And, remember, "There's always room for one more!

VAYETZE (WE ARE ALL HUMAN)

The book of Genesis is chock-full of Torah portions that have so much going on in them that any one of them would make for great soap opera content. This week's Torah portion – *Vayetze*, which means "and he left" -- is filled with deceit, trickery, polygamy, jealousy, bribery and lots of sex. The portion begins with Jacob leaving his home to live with his mother's brother, his uncle, Laban. Earlier, in this biblical episode, Jacob steals his older brother, Esau's birthright and receives the blessing of the first-born from his father, Isaac. Esau is angry and vows to kill his brother, Jacob. Fearing Esau may harm Jacob, their mother Rebecca urges Jacob to go to her brother, Laban. And, Isaac seals the deal when he blesses Jacob sending him on his way to take a wife from among the daughters of Laban. This recognizes Jacob as being the true heir of Abraham's covenant by not marrying outside the family. Confused yet? Just wait, there is more.

Not only was Jacob deceitful, but he meets his match when he joins his Uncle Laban. Jacob asks to marry his beautiful cousin, Rachel, but Laban tricks him and substitutes his older daughter, Leah instead. Laban then tells Jacob that he can marry Rachel too if he works for him for seven more years. So, now Jacob has two wives – two sisters! The sisters are jealous of one another. Leah is jealous of Rachel because Jacob loves her more and Rachel is jealous of Leah because she can bear Jacob children. Leah bears Jacob four sons – Reuven, Simeon, Levi and Judah. Rachel wants children so badly, that she gives her handmaiden, Bilhah to Jacob in marriage. This union produces two "surrogate" sons for Rachel – Dan & Naphtali. Then, not to be outdone, Leah gives her handmaiden Zilpah in marriage to Jacob and she bears two sons – Gad and Asher. Rachel trades Leah privileges to sleep with Jacob in exchange for some mandrakes, a flowering plant touted for its properties of fertility. After getting Jacob back in her bed, Leah gives birth to two more sons – Isaachar and Zebulun and a daughter, Dina. Finally, Rachel gives birth to Joseph, who becomes his father Jacob's favorite. In the next episode, Rachel dies in childbirth having Jacob's last son, Benjamin. These twelve sons of Jacob become the 12 tribes of Israel.

It is somewhat disturbing that our ancestors behaved this badly -- there was hate, jealousy, distrust, bribery, the list goes on and on. But perhaps the lesson to be learned here is that we <u>can</u> learn from their mistakes. We are able to see that these behaviors are not becoming and are often punished. We are also given laws by God later in the Torah that discourage and even prohibit many of these poor behaviors. We do stand on the shoulders of our ancestors, and we can learn from both their successes and their shortcomings. We are all human, we all make mistakes. But, we can choose not to repeat these mistakes, to try to be better, to forgive and not hold grudges and to be the best person we can be. Amen.

VAYIGASH (70 WAYS TO LOOK AT TORAH)

This Shabbat, we read from Genesis, Chapters 44-47. It is one of the very few Torah portions that begins in the middle of a chapter. At the end of the previous portion, we are left hanging like a "to be continued" television episode. We do not know what will happen to Benjamin, what will become of his brothers, or what will become of their father, Jacob? In *Vayigash*, many questions are answered and prophesies are resolved.

Joseph reveals himself to his brothers and tells them that he was meant to be in Egypt so that he could ensure the survival of his family. He sends his brothers back to Canaan to gather their father and their "children and grandchildren, flocks and herds, and all that is [theirs]." He tells them that they shall dwell in Egypt in the region of Goshen and that they will be taken care of. This event of our patriarchs and matriarchs moving to Egypt is said to be the fulfillment of God's prophecy to Abraham in Genesis Chapter 15 that his "offspring shall be strangers in a land not theirs, they shall be enslaved and oppressed,....but I will execute judgment on the nation they shall serve and in the end they shall go free with great wealth."

It is said that the total of Jacob's household who came to Egypt was seventy people. The number seventy is used often in the Torah. It is a symbolic number signifying totality or completeness.

The *Mishnah* tells us that there are seventy facets of Torah. Some commentators equate these seventy members of Jacob's family with the seventy facets of Torah. We are taught that we can spend a lifetime studying the Torah and never see all the different sides of it. It is like peeling an onion, there are so many layers to uncover. It is said, too, that the seventy members of Jacob's family who went to dwell in Goshen represented every type of Jew, "from the holiest to the most remote" (*Likutey Halachot, Sukkah 6:12*). These are the ancestors of our Jewish people, all types – and because of them, we are here to continue the traditions and practices of the Jewish people.

We are told that there are seventy different ways of <u>looking</u> at the Torah and there are seventy different types of Jews that we are descended from. It is interesting to note that when we "<u>look</u>" at something, we use our eyes. The Hebrew word for eye is *Ayin*. There is also a Hebrew letter named *Ayin* whose numerical value happens to be the number 70. May we always have the curiosity to <u>look</u> at the Torah and our world in many different ways, always striving to bring out the best in ourselves, in others and for the good of our world. Amen.

VAYISHLACH (I HAVE ALL)

As I was reading some of the commentaries on this Torah portion, there were some interesting opinions about Genesis Chapter 33, verses 9-11 when Esau and Jacob reunite. Remember, Jacob has fled his home after stealing his older brother Esau's birthright and fearing that Esau might harm him. Now Jacob wants to give Esau some of his flock as a peace offering. Esau replies, "I have PLENTY (ENOUGH)…let what you have remain yours." Jacob again insists that Esau accept his gift by saying, "Please accept my present…for God has favored me and I have ALL (EVERYTHING)."

Many commentators make a distinction between the different use of words by Esau and Jacob. Esau says he has plenty or enough. "Plenty" is a quantitative word indicating that Esau has material possessions and this is what is important to him. However, Jacob arrives to meet Esau with his entire family and states, "I have all." This implies that Jacob's possessions are his family and this is everything to him.

Our society and the media put so much emphasis on the physical or material things that we possess and the successes and achievements we gain in our lives. But, are these really the things that are most valuable and important to us?

If you visit a cemetery, you will find that most of the headstones do not list the possessions or personal achievements of the deceased. Instead, they state the virtues the deceased possessed as a parent, a friend, a sibling or a spouse.

So often we get wrapped up in the world of material possessions and how we can increase the value of our resume, that we forget what is really important. Sometimes it takes a "wake-up call" to realize that family and dear friends are our greatest wealth. If we only concentrate on the material things, we will never be satisfied or have enough. There is always more that we can have and more that we can strive to achieve. But if we cherish the priceless things we have in our lives – our family and friends - we will always be full and we will, like Jacob, have everything we need. Amen.

YIZKOR (EVERYONE HAS A NAME)

Zelda Schneersohn Mishkowsky was born in Poland in 1914. When she was 12 years old, her family immigrated to Israel. Zelda's father was the great, great grandson of the 3rd Lubavitcher Rebbe, Manachem Schneersohn. Zelda devoted her life to writing and teaching writing. She died in 1984 and is best remembered for her poetry. In 1968, she published what is perhaps her most famous poem – *L'chol Ish Yeh Shem* – Everyone Has A Name.

This poem has become the centerpiece of Yom Hashoah ceremonies in Israel since 1989 when the Worldwide Holocaust Memorial Project began. In Israel, *Yom Hashoah* is a national day of commemoration - a day which memorializes the 6 million Jews murdered in the Holocaust. Each year, on the evening of the 27th day of *Nisan*, a special ceremony is held at *Yad Vashem*, the living memorial to the Holocaust in Israel. During the evening ceremony, six torches are lit commemorating the six million Jews who perished. On the following morning, a siren is sounded for 2 minutes and for the duration of that time, everything stops. People cease working, traffic comes to a halt and everyone stands in silence and reverence to the victims of the Holocaust. At the Knesset, the seat of government in Israel, Zelda's poem is read and the names of those who perished are read aloud. The public recitation of these names on *Yom Hashoah* perpetuates their memory and restores their identity and their dignity.

After the Holocaust, the Reform movement decided that everyone would rise and say *Kaddish* even if they did not have a *Yahrzeit* of a loved one. In this way, there would always be someone to say *Kaddish* for those who had no one to say *Kaddish* for them. By taking responsibility for saying *Kaddish* for them, we honor them. Each of those 6 million who perished in the Holocaust was a person, an individual with a personal story…a story that began with a name.

In our own community, we are in the process of erecting a memorial to those who were murdered in the Holocaust. This is a community effort and each and every person in our Temple and our community at large has an opportunity to donate to the creation of this memorial. It will be located in downtown Alexandria near Rapides Regional Medical Center. I hope you will participate by donating to this project which will remember the names of those whose lives were cut short in the Holocaust. Their individual stories began with a name and will end with our remembrance of them always through this memorial.

♪ ♪ Everyone has a name given by God

    Given by our parents
    By our stature, given by our smile.
    Given by the clothes we wear
    Given by the mountains
    Given by our walls.
    By the planets
    Given by our neighbors
    By our sins, our longing.
    Everyone has a name
    Given by our enemies
    Given by our love
    Our rejoicing, given by our labor.
    Everyone has a name
    Given by the seasons
    Given by our blindness
    By the sea, our death.
    L'chol ish yeh shem
    Everyone has a name
    Given by God, given by our parents
    Everyone has a name
    L'chol ish yeh shem.

                    Melody by Benjie Ellen Schiller

YOM KIPPUR

On *Rosh Hashanah* and *Yom Kippur* we are reminded of not only our mortality, but also of the awesomeness of each and every day we are given on this earth. In one of the Torah portions which we read on *Yom Kippur* – *Acharei Mot* – Adonai instructs Moses to tell Aaron that he must not enter the sanctuary. Aaron is only allowed to enter the Holy of Holies once a year on *Yom Kippur*. Rashi interprets this to mean that if Aaron could enter the Sanctuary anytime he wanted to, the specialness of the Sanctuary and the job he was tasked to do as High Priest would eventually wear off. The grandeur and spirituality would wane and his duties might become mundane. But, by only entering the Sanctuary once a year, Aaron would never lose the awe and the importance of his duties.

We often joke about people who only come to services once or twice a year – on the High Holy Days. But, perhaps if we look at this in a more positive way we might understand that they too are experiencing the awe and specialness of this time of year. If they came to services all the time, would attendance during the High Holy Days be as special?

And what about those of us who do attend regularly? Just as we must strive to see each day anew, we also have the power to see the Holy Days as special. Because they only come once a year, they are special and there are rituals that they offer which are new and different than those we experience on a regular Shabbat.

May we all embrace the newness and specialness of these High Holy Days. May we as rabbis continue to make *Rosh Hashanah* and *Yom Kippur* special for both those who attend regularly and those who attend only once or twice a year. We should all look at each and every new day as a blessing and search for fresh experiences to make each day special in our lives. Amen.

NURTURING OUR SOULS: DISCOVERING OUR PURPOSE

This paper will concentrate on our souls, discussing various definitions of a soul and how we, as human beings, find our purpose or destiny in life. It will also discuss how we, as clergy, nurture our souls in order to live a purposeful and meaningful life ultimately contributing to *Tikkun Olam*.

I personally believe that human beings consist of four primary parts: our **body**, our **mind**, our **heart** and our **soul**.

Our Body

Our body is the vessel or container that gives us our shape and form. Our body makes us all different from one another and our body has the ability to change over time as we age, as we gain or lose weight, as we deal with sickness or injury or as some choose to change their body by artificial means. Our body is not that important in a spiritual sense. It is merely a shell or container. Unfortunately, our society puts so much emphasis on how we physically look, and so much attention is given to our body. But, does it really matter how fat or thin we are? How young we look? What color our hair is, or if we have hair? Remember, "Beauty is in the eyes of the beholder" and "Beauty is only skin deep." What is beautiful to one person, may not be beautiful to another person. And, although someone has a beautiful "outside", they may not have a beautiful inside to match it. It is what is inside of us that really matters. Of course, we should take general care of our body by eating well, exercising and not abusing our body with drugs or participating in activities that can be harmful. This is not always easy, and sometimes our body needs to rely on the other parts of us to be the best they can be. After all, a body cannot make decisions. But, our body and our features make us each unique whether we accept them as they were given or make adjustments for what we might feel is better. Our body is only a container. It holds all that we are in human form.

Our Mind

Our mind allows us to think, learn, discover, create, decide, dream, doubt and judge. Everyone's mind does not have the same capacity. But we should all use our mind to the best of our abilities. As the saying goes, "A mind is a terrible thing to waste." With our short time on this earth, we should use our mind to learn and discover as much as we can. And then, we must use our mind to share our discoveries and knowledge with others. Part of our learning and discovering is to find our individual purpose in life. What are we here for? What can we leave as a legacy? What can we do to participate in *tikkun olam* – repair of the world? Everyone does not do everything well, but everyone does something well. Part of our journey on this earth is to discover what we do well and once discovered, we must share this with the world. In this way, we discover our destiny or purpose, and we

can make the world a better place because we were in it. God gives each of us unique gifts. And, we give back to God, our creator, when we are able to discover these gifts and share them with others. Our mind is an engine of discovery. It keeps us going. It allows us to learn, grow, choose and share.

Our Heart

Our heart allows us to love or deny love. Within our heart lies a tangle of emotions. If our heart is free, we are able to love unconditionally. If our heart is hardened, we live with a heaviness from which we are not free. Only we can decide how we react to things around us. We can choose to act with love or we can choose to act with hate. We can choose to laugh and we can choose to cry. We can choose to look at the world as a glass half full or a glass half empty. Our heart is a thermostat. It regulates emotions and responds with reactions. We choose how we set our personal thermostat. We can be hot or we can be cold. We can be warm and loving or we can be cold and hateful.

Our Soul

Our soul is a tiny piece of our creator given to each and every one of us. Without this spark of life or light, we would not exist. We cannot see our soul and we have no control over it. Our soul is pure. Through our soul, we are all on an even playing field. Each soul is a spark of the creator..the part of us that is *B'tzelem Elohim*…made in the image of God. Rabbi Manis Friedman, a well-known and prolific Chabad lecturer, says that the soul is "a little piece of life." No matter what we do on this earth – good or bad – our soul always remains pure. It cannot be altered, it cannot be shut down, it cannot be stifled. It is a living thing. The soul never dies. It lives on after our bodies, our minds and our hearts are gone. The soul returns to God who gave it (Eccl. 12:7). Our soul is a barometer. It allows us to react to what goes on around us. It is our conscience, our destiny and our destination – always good, always guiding us to do the right and purposeful thing if we only listen to it.

We are all connected through our souls. We can visualize this using the image of a wheel. We all live our own individual lives in our individual bodies making choices with our minds and our hearts. Each one of us is a spoke in the wheel. At the rim or outer part of the wheel, each spoke is disconnected and separate. But at the hub, the center, the core, all of the spokes connect. This core is our spiritual hub. It illustrates how we all come from the same source…our souls are all connected. We can change every part of ourselves, but not our soul. We can change our body, we can change our mind, and we can even change the feelings of our heart, but we cannot change anything about the soul. The soul is pure and given from God. The soul is our guiding light. Our job is to listen to it and to find that light which will lead us to our unique purposeful life on this earth.

Our soul is the essence – the real "us". All the rest is decoration. We must learn to listen to our soul. We must be able to hush the desires of the mind, the body and the heart in order to hear and know our true purpose in life. Our soul is a guiding light, leading us to do what we were put on this earth to do. Unfortunately, the majority of human beings never really live out their life's purpose or find the true destiny of their soul. I know I am one of the lucky ones who were able to figure out early in life what my purpose was. I try to live a purposeful life each and every day. I hope that the world will be a better place because I was in it.

Soul Stories

There is a Kabbalistic teaching that all the souls of the world are contained in one body – *Adam ha-rishon*. Whenever a person is born, they are assigned a particular soul which already knows the destiny or purpose of the human being it is assigned to.

In the Babylonian Talmud, we are taught: "As God fills the whole world, so also the soul fills the whole body. As God sees, but cannot be seen, so also the soul sees, but cannot be seen. As God nourishes the whole world, so also the soul nourishes the whole body. As God is pure, so also the soul is pure. As God dwells in the innermost part of the Universe, so also the soul dwells in the innermost part of the body."

Rabbi Manis Friedman makes a very interesting speculation. He believes that every soul goes through the "valley of the shadow of death." According to Rabbi Friedman, this "valley" of the shadow of death is the birth process and this is what is referred to in the 23rd Psalm. It is the blank space between life inside the womb and life outside the womb. He explains that every birth is a near death experience. We survive birth because God is there to help us experience it.

In his book, <u>Before You Were Born</u>, author, Howard Schwartz retells the Midrash of the angel, Lailah, who brings the soul and the seed together and then sees to it that the seed is planted in the womb. In doing so, Lailah serves as a midwife of souls. While the infant grows in the womb, Lailah teaches the unborn child the entire Torah, as well as the history of his or her own soul. Then, the instant the child is born, the angel lightly strikes its finger to the child's lip, as if to say "shh," and this causes the child to forget everything learned in the womb. This myth provides an explanation of the origin of the mysterious indentation every person has on their upper lip. It is our job to strive to re-learn all we were taught. The myth goes on to say that the angel Lailah watches over the child all of his days, serving as a guardian angel. And when the time comes for a person to take leave of this world, Lailah leads him from this world into the next.

In the *Zohar* (the main book concerning the secrets of Jewish mysticism, called *Kabbalah*), the soul is often described as having three qualities or levels: *neshamah*, *ruach* and *nefesh*. The deepest, innermost level (what I like to call the seed) is the **neshamah** – the spark deep inside that is given to us by Adonai. It is the *neshamah* that we speak of in our liturgy when we recite, "*Elohai neshamah shenatata bi t'horah hi.*" "The soul that You have given me, O God, is pure."

This *neshamah* or spark is brought to life by a flame - **ruach** – the spirit or breath of Adonai. Just as a fire can only burn if there is air, our *neshamah* can only come to life if we connect to Adonai in some way. We must find and feel God's breath/spirit or *ruach* within us. Shabbat is a wonderful time to make a connection to Adonai. Shabbat, if we let it, can force us to stop and quiet ourselves – to help us be in the moment with our God. Shabbat can be a time to ignite the flame of our *neshamah* where we can choose to participate in study gaining new knowledge, meditation or silence helping us to understand ourselves and how we fit into the world, or just doing something that is different from what we do on all the other work days of our week.

Surrounding the flame of *ruach* is the level of soul known as **nefesh**. *Nefesh* is the level of the soul that connects the spiritual and physical parts of our selves. We can visualize all of this as a candle within a hurricane glass. The candle is the *neshamah*. The candle flame is the *ruach*. And the *nefesh* is the hurricane glass which protects it. The light of our souls is fueled by breath (air) and is protected by our bodies. We should be careful not to take breath for granted. For each breath brings life. Each breath can be healing, cleansing, renewing -- changing us as we allow ourselves to be changed. Each time we breathe, we should be reminded of the fragility of life and our life's purpose. With each breath we take, we <u>can</u> connect to Adonai and become filled with God's *ruach* enabling our *neshamah* to shine and our *nefesh* to find its greater purpose in the world.

Finding Our Purpose

Through the years I have dabbled in the study of Numerology. According to Numerology, we all choose our parents, our name and the particular date on which we are born into this world. In Numerology, you use the numbers that correspond to your given birth name and the numbers of your date of birth to determine specific things about your personality, your deepest desires and your destiny or purpose. It is uncanny how many times I have done a Numerology chart for someone I know and it describes them perfectly. In an essay, storyteller, Peninnah Schram shares that "According to the Jewish tradition, names are important for identification and family history, and, more essentially, for revelation of the soul or essence of the individual." The Talmud teaches that there are three names by which a person is called: "one which their parents call them, one which people (others) call them, and one which they earn for themselves. The last is the best one of all." I do believe that the soul is our essence. It is our destiny, what we share with this world and what we are remembered for. It is the name we earn for ourselves. We are all put on this earth for a purpose. If we live a fulfilling and purposeful life, we have discovered our purpose and we are able to share it for the good of others. The ultimate question of life is, "What is your soul calling you to do?"

In their book, Whistle While You Work, authors Richard Leider and David Shapiro define our purpose in life or our "calling" as "an inner urge to give our gifts away." According to them, we are all born with God given gifts to fulfill a specific purpose on this earth. These gifts have the potential to enrich our lives if they are unwrapped and shared. We must listen to our calling because our calling will make a difference in the world and can be our legacy when we leave this world.

In her wonderful book, The Renaissance Soul, Margaret Lobenstine helps us find ways to make our dreams come true. She encourages us to discover our passions – what we truly LOVE to do – and find ways to make a living sharing our passions. We have to love what we do. My philosophy has always been, "You must love what you do each and every day. If you do not, then find something else to do." In order to live your true destiny, you must be passionate about what you do. We should not be willing to just accept what life gives us. We must always be searching for why things happen and how we can rise above the curve balls that life throws us. I believe that everything happens for a reason. We may not always understand the reason, especially when bad things happen. But as time goes on, we have the ability to eventually learn lessons that make our understanding clearer. We have to be able to move beyond the trials and tribulations of life finding ways to be in control of our lives…finding ways to share our unique gifts with others to make this world a better place.

In the fall of 2005, the Louisiana coast was hit by the most devastating hurricane in our history – Hurricane Katrina. Thousands of people lost everything. I was privileged to be able to work with many of these people helping them get over their anger, grief and fear and ultimately discover a new place of healing and hope. I was amazed by how little anger I saw from people who could have chosen to be very angry. What had happened to them was not fair. Instead, most of them chose to find ways to move forward with faith, hope and community instead of dwelling in the past and feeling angry or sorry for themselves. They knew that there was a higher purpose and they were willing to patiently learn how and where to discover it. I learned a great deal from the Katrina evacuees. Even in the most devastating of situations, there is always hope, there is always something better, there is always promise. It is our choice and our purpose to continually strive to find it within our own individual lives.

Interestingly enough, St. Benedict is quoted as saying, "To work is to pray." The Hebrew word *avodah* literally means "work", but it can also mean "service to God" or prayer. In this way, what we do for a living, our life's work, has a very spiritual connection. Even more reason to love what we do.

Nurturing Our Souls

So, how do we as clergy nurture our souls? Most clergy are "on call" 24 hours a day, seven days a week. They must be able to drop what they are doing at a moment's notice, return from vacations or special events with their families and often put the needs of others in front of their own. I, for one, seem to thrive on this. It has always been in my nature to help others. Most of the time I do put the needs of others before my own and I think nothing of it. I think part of it is the culture I grew up in. My family was always giving to others, opening their home to those who needed them, volunteering in the community and advocating leadership by example. This is what I saw each and every day. So, it makes sense that I would be very comfortable giving to other people, to my community and to my faith. My favorite quote and motto has always been: "You shouldn't go through life with a catcher's mitt on both hands. You need to be able to throw something back."

I feel that part of my purpose in this life is to share the gift of my singing voice with others. Each and every time I sing, I feel that I am taken to a special place. I feel as if God is singing through me, urging me to share the beautiful gift I have been given. I also feel a calling to share the spirituality I feel with Judaism…to create meaningful liturgy and life cycle events and to be a good and compassionate listener. These are things that feed my soul. Many of my colleagues say that they cannot pray or feel God when they are leading a service. I feel just the opposite. If I am truly there in the moment, I feel as if I am a conduit sharing the songs and writings of our faith in a spiritual and meaningful way. If I cannot feel it myself, how can others? Now, there are rare times when everything does not come together like it should. But, I can honestly say, for the most part, when I am involved in leading a service or performing a life cycle event, my soul is being fed and I am getting something spiritually out of it. This is one reason I wanted to be a part of JSLI. It offered a way for me to become more "official" in sharing my Jewish gifts.

In addition, I happen to be a Certified Sound Healer using vibrations from tuning forks and the sound of my voice to relax and heal. When I work on a client, I am also (indirectly) being healed. And, one of the most important things I do is sing at the bedside of the dying. It is at these times that I know there is a God. It may sound strange to say, but this is one of the most rewarding things I have done in life. There is nothing more satisfying than knowing that you have helped someone be at peace and consequently brought some measure of peace to their loved ones as well.

There are several other ways that I personally nurture my soul. I love to learn and I hope to never stop learning. I love music, especially music from the Baroque period and the pure sounds of Bel Canto. I can truly be taken to another place when I hear this type of music. And, I love to sing…anytime I am singing, my soul is nurtured. And, sometimes, I love silence….silence where you listen to the sounds around you and the sounds of your own body and soul. It is at these times when I become most creative. It is interesting to note that the words "silence" and "listen" contain the exact same letters. This is NOT a coincidence. We must be silent in order to listen. And, we must listen often both to others and ourselves. To me, this is an important part of being a member of the clergy. Being silent and listening helps us to connect with others, and also to connect with our own inner being and soul.

As part of this thesis, I thought it would be interesting to survey a number of clergy, both Jewish and non-Jewish asking them 2 basic questions. I think their answers are food for thought and fascinating. As I commented to one of the non-Jewish clergy, "It is amazing how our faiths can be so different, yet our concept of the soul so similar. If only everyone could look at how similar we are and not dwell on the differences, our world would be a better (and more peaceful) place." I include this as an appendix to this paper. The two questions posed to clergy were:

1) How do you define our "soul?"

2) As clergy, we are so busy nurturing the souls of others....How do you nurture or take care of your own soul? How do you take time to do this? What are your results? Please elaborate.

Appendix

Below are the responses to the two questions. Each individual person's response is separated by a bullet dot and their responses to the two questions are shown as two separate paragraphs.

- *N'shama*, soul and *N'sheema*, breath, are connected. As we deepen our breath, we can begin to connect to the universe within us and begin to hear the still, small voice within, which is really our soul. Our soul is the spirit within us that has no body, has no limitations or form. It is our free form being which will exist in the spirit world long after our body expires. *Cantor Lisa Levine*

    Mainly, I practice yoga. Through the practice of slowing my breath, meditating and practicing asanas, I nurture that still, small voice and listen to what my soul is telling me.

Often it is hard to hear our own needs and desires because they are eclipsed by chatter and and busy work. By taking time to go to the mat, I create a *mishkan*, a holy space for myself to unwind and listen to what my soul is saying. This also relieves stress, strengthens my body and brings my mind into focus. The results are that I am more invigorated, calm and able to help others more effectively. I can also pray with greater intention, sing with greater power and give more of myself to others without losing myself. Another way I nurture my soul is through working the land. I have an extensive garden and spend eight months of the year growing food. From the first seeds in March to the final harvest in October, gardening is much akin to life. We plant a seed in the ground, water it and hope that it sprouts. Then we weed the sprouts so that the plants will grow strong. This is hard to do, because once you see a seedling, you don't want to pull it. But in order for the other plants to grow strong, you must sacrifice and thin the seeds. [It is] the same in life. If you take on too much, everything suffers. You watch the seedling grow into a plant and get flowers, sure sign of fruit. When the fruit finally comes on you rejoice. You wait patiently until the fruit is ripe. Then on the day you want to harvest, you see that something has come and eaten your crop. This is devastating. But such is life. Sometimes all your work is in vain. Things don't always work out the way you plan. But then you plant another seed, water it and wait. Life is like that too. Our souls are ultimately at the mercy of the higher power. We are not in control. The key is to learn how to cope with the changes, the losses, the disappointments. Nurturing one's soul can help with that. Music helps too. I love to use chant and repetitive music to nurture my soul. It soothes and calms, renews and releases stress. *Cantor Lisa Levine*

- The unknown entity that binds us to G-D. *Cantor Don Croll*

I nurture my soul by reading the extra readings in our prayer book. I rarely take time to do this. It happens spontaneously when I'm looking for something and a reading catches my eye. I sometimes find these readings during the silent prayer. I stop and marvel at the beautiful poetry or essay. There is a sense of peace within me. *Cantor Don Croll*

- I choose to take Genesis literally where it says God breathed life into the nostrils of Adam and Adam became a living creature. The term "*n'shamah*" for breath is also a term for "soul". So, I choose to believe that my soul is God's breath within me. And, when I die, stop breathing, my soul/breath returns to its source, to God. I also lean toward the 9th century teachings of the *Chaidei Ashkenaz* who hold that our souls are here to serve a task given them by God and helps fulfill God's plan. When we've done what we're supposed to do, this time around no matter how long or short a time it is, we return to God's presence and wait till we are needed again. Not punishment or karma of Eastern traditions, but rather blessed, useful purposes. So, my soul is here to carry out God's plan, though I don't know what that is nor am I always sure about what I'm doing. None the less, I keep trying. *Rabbi James Kessler*

My soul is nurtured by what I do for others and for the Jewish people. My problem is, how do I nurture my body in a manner that it can keep doing what the soul needs to be carried out? That's the problem for me. My soul is doing fine; my body and mind need attention. I'm terrible at doing that. I've try dozens of things from yoga to mysticism to a few drugs in the past, to booze now and

then, to meditation to *Musar*. Some work for a while and then become useless. At 68, I guess I'll just keep trying. I am, however, very rejuvenated in spirit by what I do, even when it fails. I learn from screw ups.
Rabbi James Kessler

- I believe the "soul" is the Divine essence within each human being that makes us holy and allows us to do God's work here on earth. *Anonymous*

Regarding nurturing our own souls, first is to make sure to have time for ourselves and our families away from the Temple, etc. A day off should be sacred and interrupted only for emergencies. Then we should also find ways to infuse our own passions into our congregations and find opportunities to conduct services in a way that we personally find moving spiritually even if it is different from the congregational norm. For myself I am moved spiritually when we bring in outside talent, especially a musician, who changes up the service in a way that makes it much more spiritually enjoyable and less like work from time to time. *Anonymous*

- Our soul is our very being. It is our immaterial essence. It is what animates us, what gives us emotions. It is the spiritual center in every human being. *Cantor Jessica Roskin*

In a way, my ability to nurture the souls of my congregation gives me a deep feeling of satisfaction and therefore nurtures my own soul. But, I do understand the question. As satisfying as it is, it can also be draining. When I am able to separate myself and take some time to walk around a peaceful, beautiful place like a botanical gardens on a sunny day, or read a good book and insert

myself into its reality and out of mine; to spend time with people I love and share a good meal whether I or someone else cooked it, or even to get a massage, which I try to do regularly, are ways I nurture my own soul. All of those activities give me a sense of peace and contentment.
Cantor Jessica Roskin

- The soul is that within us which is permanent and is no longer within us when we die. It is as the Hebrew implies, *neshamah*, "the breath" of life. It is that which *inspires* us (just as the word "inspire" and "inspiration" are themselves derived from the act of "breathing in") as we live and is expired (that is, "breathed out") when we are no longer extant. In this sense, our soul is shared with all life, sentient and insentient. And, in this sense, it returns to our Creator as pure as it came into us. For me, this is the meaning of the idea that the soul is given to us "pure" and God wishes us to return it "pure." We defile the soul by doing that which pollutes our atmosphere physically and morally. Of course, the use of the word "defile" is extreme. No one lives who does not sin. This is the nature of an imperfect world. So the struggle for the whole person, body and soul, is to overcome the urge to do that which is sinful, to learn to use the *yetzer hara* in constructive ways that enrich our atmosphere, our families, our friends, our neighbors, our community, our people, our species, and even our world. If the soul is unique in some way, I think it is only the same uniqueness that inheres in every blade of grass or every drop of water in the ocean. No two souls are alike, yet none forms a person in and of itself. Only for that brief period when body and soul are joined does the chemistry of soul take on meaning in our human context. Even then, we are always part of something larger than ourselves and never

can gain sufficient perspective to know exactly what that something is. The richness of life is gaining perspective, seeking more and more knowledge—coming to know ourselves and others, coming to know the world around us, and glimpsing the divine. Obviously the soul's part in this is crucial, but so is mind and body.
Rabbi Seymour Rossel

I nurture my "soul" through enjoying my family, celebrating life, study, discourse, and dialogue with my closest colleagues. Besides, I find the idea that one can become empty by nurturing others a bit self-serving. I believe we can only nurture others to the extent that they can take in what we have to offer, but that never diminishes what we have to offer. If the body needs a vacation, that's understandable. But it is inconceivable to me to speculate that somehow my soul needs a break. I think there's a long one coming and I do not plan to rush that one at all. *Rabbi Seymour Rossel*

- Our soul is the innermost spark that makes us human beings. It contains our rhythm, our consciousness and our directional guide. It helps us connect to ourselves, to others and to the Divine. *Cantor Robbi Sherwin*

I am so blessed in that I have the energy, ability and gifts - that I do not take lightly - to be able to share with others. My band, *Sababa*, fills my soul with such richness - I can't begin to express what it does to be able to share sacred times and moments with others through our music. In my work composing music, writing, leading retreats or Shabbaton and finding God through nature, I make sure that I carve out some time for myself. I retreat yearly with several colleagues in the wilderness - rafting, camping and exploring. I also truly love meeting with my cantorial colleagues through the Women Cantors' Network, who spark me with their ideas and shared challenges. I cannot say enough about how important it is to have peers that you trust and look up to, and peers with whom you can share. I make sure that I exercise to keep my body and mind in balance. I am aware of what I put in my body, so as to nurture it to be healthy. I believe that body and soul are deeply connected, and if one is healthy, the other can find a way to be, as well. I make sure I surround myself with good friends, a weekly few hours of mah jong and make nights to be with my family. I turn down other opportunities to do so - taking better care of me helps me take better care of others. *Cantor Robbi Sherwin*

- I rarely use the word "soul" either in conversation or writing, or, when I was preaching, in sermon. My mind automatically translates a term back into Hebrew where I am, in such matters, more comfortable. So there you have two words, twice the question: *nefesh* נפש and *n'shamah* נשמה. Both words suggest breathing. My teacher Reb Zalman said *n'shamah* was "inhale" and *nefesh* is "exhale." A third term, *ruach* רוח is "spirit," which ties together the two terms for "soul" because *ruach* basically is "wind." (Check out the etymology of "spirit.") So, through this exercise, "soul" means "life," or perhaps, "the essence of life." It would be a universal characteristic of living beings, a life force, an appetite for existence. Differences between one person's soul and another person's soul would be a matter of culture and experience. That being said, I do use the word "soul," to refer to an innermost place, self-consciousness, maybe, or "gut." An example would be

"music reaches the soul," or better yet (easier for me to comprehend), "the sense of smell goes directly to the soul." (I like the association of "smell" with breathing.)
Rabbi David Kline

Two activities leap to mind when it comes to my nurturing my soul: eating and study. Barbara, my wife, and I are confirmed foodies. We obsess on food aesthetics and nutrition, preparation and enjoyment. (Could be that this comes up first because it is getting close to dinner time and I am going to make pasta by hand.) Study is what I do, and it includes teaching and writing. Nurturing my soul is gratification and I have done a lot of that over the years, including reading (novels, plays, poetry), jogging, walking, cycling, making and listening to music, dance, meditation and praying. *Rabbi David Kline*

- To me, the soul is the animated part of our being. It's the limitless divine-ness of our limited mortal existence. *Rabbi Marshal Klaven*

To be honest, I focus on the small things: dinners with my wife, walks with my dog, exercise 3-4 times per week, and text study with my co-workers 1-2 month. Though, I seem to miss these goals regularly, it has worked best by putting them on the schedule (considering them sacred, reserved time). I focus on the small things, because the large thing which reinvigorates my soul time and time again is working with my communities! It's all I need. *Rabbi Marshal Klaven*

- I would say the soul is the part of us that makes us unique and that is created in God's image. *Anonymous*

This is something that I had to learn how to do. Being a rabbi of a congregation or a chaplain is very draining and we need to learn self-care. I have found it important to have my own space for prayer--the candles Friday night, the silent *Amida*, asking reflective questions of the congregation and answering them myself--these are important times for me. Self-care is more than prayer--it is making your family a priority. For me, that includes never working on Seder nights outside of our home, not working every Friday night (I know that this is not always possible, but I was able to do it). Having colleagues to talk to when I am in need of friendship or counsel is very important also. Finally, a good working relationship with a community that appreciated me and supported me made 25 years with them pass quickly. *Anonymous*

- The soul is that part of us that goes beyond just a kind heart or a sweet character. The soul is our very essence. It is that part of us that makes our eyes glisten when we hear of someone else's accomplishments. It is that part of us that makes a difference in someone else's life without even being conscious of the gift that we are giving. It is that part of our character that separates us and makes us stand out as uniquely blessed by God. *Cantor Rachelle Nelson*

It isn't easy to find the time to take care of our own souls and therefore, our calling to give to others has to fill us up with so much meaning that we are replenished by the *mitzvot* that we do. We also need to be able to go to those places, whether physically or emotionally that fill us up with joy and rejuvenate us. For me, I go to my children, my garden where I grow vegetables and plant, and to my animals which give me unconditional love. I find that the gifts that God has given me will often nurture my soul and rejuvenate it. *Cantor Rachelle Nelson*

- Once when I was speaking to my Religious School students about the soul, one of them said, "The soul is what makes you you." Beyond the Jewish definitions of the levels/definitions of the soul, I really still like that description. My soul is....my essence - what makes me who I am. *Anonymous*

I try to read books that give me ideas that are inspiring, especially books about God and the interconnections in the Universe that reflect God. I sing and listen to music I find meaningful. I write new songs to express myself, or sing my own songs for that personal expression. I make sure that my writings, *Divrei Torah* and articles for our Temple newsletter express the depth of my feelings in some way. I try to make my study with congregants go beyond the simple meaning of the text in order to relate it to real life. *Anonymous*

- Our *nefesh* is not a physical thing. I can't point to it, but yet I can feel it. It motivates me and it guides me. My *nefesh* is where God resides in me. I believe that we are all connected to God via our *nefesh*. God is everything, God is everywhere, God is the good in our world and yes, God is even in the evil of our world. God gave us (humanity) free will. My *nefesh* was here before me and my *nefesh* will go back to God when my physical body dies. Our son Aron is exactly like my grandfather with very few exceptions. Yet, they never physically met. Our body is only a vessel to contain or represent our *nefesh* while we are here in the physical world. After we depart this world our *nefesh* returns to God where for the lack of a better word it is

recycled or continued via another person yet unborn. Our *nefesh* is what defines us. It is who we are.
Rabbi Barry Altmark

Hopefully, this does not sound like I'm avoiding the direct question. By nurturing others I am fulfilling what I was meant to do. Huh? I am a nurturer, that's what I do. I want to make a better life for my wife, my son and me. Not via physical objects, although I like my toys like anybody else. When I am approached as a Rabbi it is not my job to help people, it is my duty. That's how I think, feel and operate. But, we seem to get so busy helping others and nurturing them that sometimes it feels like we leave ourselves behind or do we? It is in my being, my *nefesh* to help others. Whether, it's leading Shabbat for a congregation or feeding the homeless I must help others. It's really not a conscience choice. It is part of who I am. Having said this, sometimes I can over extend myself physically and emotionally helping others. It happens way too often and I found myself looking to recharge or reconnect with God. Me, just me! My release or escape (however you want to look at it) is via my artwork. I go to the mountains - just me and my cameras. No one else is invited. Well, someone else is invited, God. It can be on top of the mountain, it might be next to a river or just a picnic table in a campground - just me, my cameras, sometimes my favorite music playing too loud in my ears. Sometimes it takes a little while but the connection usually occurs pretty quickly. The conversation starts - just me and God. It's always been a one sided conversation, just me doing the talking or is it? God is always listening so is it really only a one sided conversation? I'm going to assume that we had the conversation because after all is said and done I leave the mountains with pretty images that speak to me and hopefully others and most importantly I've cleared the cobwebs in my head. For lack of a better term, I've been to my "Happy Place" and ready to go back into the world and assist others - just like I am meant to do. *Rabbi Barry Altmark*

- I define "soul" as the essence of who I am. It is my personality. It is my mental and emotional makeup. It's what makes me unique. I guess I take more of the traditional Christian/Greek view in that I see humans as body, soul, and spirit. The body is what makes me a physical being and connects me to the physical world. The spirit is what makes me a spiritual being and connects me to the spiritual world. It is the soul that gives me the ability to interact in both. I see people die on a weekly, if not daily basis. The body dies. That physical connection to this world ends. The ability for the soul to interact in the world stops, but I do not believe the soul ends or ceases to exist. I believe that part lives on in an afterlife. I confess I have debated within myself concerning this division of the person. I have considered the idea that I am a living, breathing, thinking, soul. I am one. There is no separation in my being. I guess the thing that causes me to question that is the aspect of death. If there is no division in my being then when death occurs everything ceases to exist; I am no more. I know some believe that, but I don't. I do try not to be so dogmatic about this that I can't consider other ways of thinking about this whole issue. *Wayne Sibley, Hospital Chaplain*

I try to spend time every day (mainly in the morning) in meditation, prayer, and scripture reading. I also spend time every week in corporate worship. Every few weeks I also try to get away, usually to my in-laws farm in North Louisiana. There I can spend time enjoying God's creation and just BE. *Wayne Sibley, Hospital Chaplain*

- I find it hard to define the soul and would rather describe it as that part of ourselves which continues to exist after we die. Thus, the concept includes an enduring historical consciousness as well as an ability to imagine the future and to be with other people in the present, but the soul also includes more, because a person who is unconscious or asleep still is or has a soul. There are also many levels of consciousness, some of which are now lost but remain nonetheless part of us. Maybe another way to describe the soul is to say that it's our essence, that part of ourselves which is free of egoistic preoccupations. *John R. Amos, Regional Vice President for Spirituality and Mission Integration, CHRISTUS Health of Central Louisiana*

I nurture my soul through reading, spiritual direction, and participating in educational experiences of a therapeutic nature. I read lots of spiritual books, books on psychology and therapy. I go to lots of workshops. I engage in therapy—on both sides of the couch. I review my life with other people on a regular basis. Sometimes other people come to me for this same review, and I am not sure whether that helps them more than it helps me. I have hobbies and have discovered that when I neglect them, I am neglecting my soul. *John R. Amos, Regional Vice President for Spirituality and Mission Integration, CHRISTUS Health of Central Louisiana*

- For me the soul is that part of our being that connects to the holy. The soul is different from and greater than the body or mind. One's soul is a lifeline to sensing and knowing the presence of the Holy One and the beauty of creation. *Pastor Lee Weems, Emmanuel Baptist Church*

I choose to nurture my soul when I take a time to observe silence and exist in the moment. The more I tune my soul to the awareness and presence of God in every moment of life then I create a reservoir when the crises come. Several years ago, I ministered to several friends in struggles and performed four funerals in two weeks time. One afternoon at the office, our minister of youth had her infant in her office. Heather allowed me to hold Hannah, rock her in my chair and be reminded that life moves forward and we live one moment at a time. Being busy uses my fuel in life; being silent and focus is my recharge time. I also use time to play for fun and enjoyment. Last week I crawled around the carpet with one of our ten month old children. As he laughed and giggled, I felt joy within. *Pastor Lee Weems, Emmanuel Baptist Church*

- To me, the soul is my breath, my voice, the stories I tell, the prayers I speak (to myself as well as to G-d), and the name I carry. In [an] essay I wrote: All of these three threads [my name, my first remembered 'Elijah' story, and the Hineni prayer of the Hazzan] share the same wellspring, namely, Jewish sacred texts and the Jewish vocal tradition. The speaking voice calling out names and telling of sacred tales, and the chanting voice singing prayers, share one thing in common: the human voice. Voice is produced by breath. Once again we have a related Hebrew word to *n'shama*, that is, *nishma*, which means both soul and breath. Therefore, when words of text are breathed, they unveil the soul. My names, the stories I remember and tell, and an inspiring storyteller's prayer intertwined and guided me to discover who I am, Peninnah the Storyteller. *Peninnah Schram*

I nourish my *neshama*/soul with the stories I read/choose/rehearse/tell because each story I find relates to me and teaches me wisdom that I need for 'choosing life'. I am also a 'hummer' - and often find myself humming *piyyutim*, melodies from a High Holy Day service, or *nigunim*. I also day dream - or meditate - for about 15 minutes during the day when I'm home. I lay down on the sofa, with soft classical music, and let my mind wander while being conscious of my breath - or even ponder on a question that is perplexing me. Good resolutions & ideas often come to me at that time. It's a form of brainstorming or riffing with myself. *Peninnah Schram*

Bibliography For Thesis

Blavin, Nehemia. *The Owner's Manual to the Soul: A Modern Guide to Spirituality from the Most Ancient Torah Sources*, Jason Aronson, 2000.

DeBenedetti, Rabbi Jana. Lecture, April 13, 2013.

Fishbane, Eitan. *The Sabbath Soul: Mystical Reflections on the Transformative Power of Holy Time*, Jewish Lights Publishing, 2012.

Frankiel, Tamar and Greenfeld, Judy. *Minding the Temple of The Soul*, Jewish Lights Publishing, 1997.

Friedman, Rabbi Manis. Lectures, *Can A Body Live Forever?* and *A Soul's Journey*.

Kedar, Karen. *God Whispers: Stories of the Soul, Lessons of the Heart*, Jewish Lights Publishing, 1999.

Laitman, Michael Rabbi. *Kabbalah for Beginners*, Kabbalah Publishers, 2007.

Leider, Richard J. and Shapiro, David A. *Whistle While You Work*, Berrett-Koehler Publishers, 2001.

Leland, Kurt. *Music and the Soul*, Hampton Roads Publishing, 2005.

Lobenstine, Margaret. *The Renaissance Soul: Life Design for People with too Many Passions to Pick Just One,* Harmony Publishing, 2006.

Matlins, Stuart, editor. *The Jewish Lights Spirituality Handbook*, Jewish Lights Publishing, 2004.

Schram, Peninnah. "The Weaver's Thread: How Name, Story, and Prayer Form the Braid of My Spiritual Life," Essay, in *Spirituality, Ethnography and Teaching: Stories From Within*. Edited by Diana Denton and Will Ashton. New York: Peter Lang Publishing, 2007.

Spitz, Elie Kaplan. *Does the Soul Survive: A Jewish Journey to Belief in Afterlife, Past Lives, and Living with Purpose*, Jewish Lights Publishing, 2001.

Schwartz, Howard. *Before You Were Born*, Roaring Brook Press, 2005.

Many thanks to my colleagues who graciously completed the survey I sent them: Rabbi Barry Altmark, John R. Amos, Cantor Don Croll, Rabbi James Kessler, Rabbi Marshall Klaven, Rabbi David Kline, Cantor Lisa Levine, Cantor Rachelle Nelson, Cantor Jessica Roskin, Rabbi Seymour Rossel, Master storyteller/educator Peninnah Schram, Cantor Robbi Sherwin, Pastor Wayne Sibley, Pastor Lee Weems and a few who wished to remain anonymous.

ABOUT THE AUTHOR

Rabbi Judy Caplan Ginsburgh is a professional singer who received a degree in Vocal Performance from the Indiana University Jacobs School of Music. She was born and raised in Alexandria, Louisiana where her family has lived since the mid-1800's. After working and living in Indiana, Illinois, Texas and Washington, DC, Judy moved back home to Louisiana in 1987.

Since 1981, Judy has made her living sharing Jewish music on pulpits throughout North America having sung in 40 of our US states and Canada. She served as cantorial soloist at Touro Synagogue in New Orleans, LA for two years and has sung as the High Holy Day soloist at B'nai Shalom in Fairfax Station, VA for fifteen years. Judy has also produced several award winning recordings of Jewish music including the best-selling *Shalom Yeladim* and *My Jewish World* which was commissioned by the URJ.

Judy is a certified sound healer and uses tuning forks, crystal bowls and vocal toning in her practice. She is also the founder and director of Central Louisiana Arts & Healthcare, Inc., a not-for-profit organization whose mission is to bring innovative arts experiences into healthcare settings to assist with the healing process. She received rabbinic ordination from the Jewish Spiritual Leaders Institute in January, 2014.

Judy's honors include: Religious Heritage of America Special Music Award, Society for the Arts in Healthcare/Blair Sadler International Healing Arts Award, National Art Education Association Award, Jubilation Award from the Tides Foundation and several Parents' Choice Awards for her recordings.

Judy lives in Louisiana with her husband, Bob. They have three children, Rachel, Aaron and Jonathan, two granddaughters, Madilyn and Marlee and a grand dog, Griffin.

www.ingramcontent.com/pod-product-compliance
Lightning Source LLC
Chambersburg PA
CBHW071731040426
42446CB00011B/2307